Social and Emotional Development

We dedicate this book to

Our first teachers, our parents:
Herb and Bea Riley
Ronaldo and Erlinda San Juan
Helen and Charles Parma
Anna and Berthold Schmied
Bill and Joan Creedon
Paul and Bridget Carns
Mary Frances Clark and Elwin Clark
Kathleen and Vincent Roach

To the teachers and directors of Wisconsin's Early Childhood Excellence Initiative, with whom we learned so many Promising Practices

And to all early childhood teachers, that may recognize their profound influence on the lives of young children as they continue on their own paths of development.

Social & emotional development

Connecting Science and Practice in Early Childhood Settings

Redleaf Press
www.redleafpress.org
800-423-8309

naeyc

Dave Riley
Robert R. San Juan
Joan Klinkner
Ann Ramminger

with

Mary Carns

Kathleen Burns

Mary A. Roach

Cindy Clark-Ericksen

Published by Redleaf Press
10 Yorkton Court
St. Paul, MN 55117
www.redleafpress.org

National Association for the
Education of Young Children
1313 L Street NW, Suite 500
Washington, DC 20005
NAEYC order number 2009

First edition 2008
Cover design by Fiona Raven
Cover photographs by Steve Wewerka
Interior typeset in Sabon and designed by Mayfly Design
Printed in the United States of America
15 14 13 12 11 10 09 08   1 2 3 4 5 6 7 8

Library of Congress Cataloging-in-Publication Data
Social and emotional development : connecting science and practice in early childhood settings / Dave Riley ... [et al.].
      p. cm.
   Includes bibliographical references and index.
   ISBN 978-1-933653-30-3 (alk. paper)
  1. Child development. 2. Child psychology. 3. Social skills. 4. Early childhood education—Activity programs. I. Riley, Dave.
   HQ767.9.S647 2007
   372.21—dc22
2007018402

Printed on acid-free paper

Social and Emotional Development

Introduction

A parent had heard that it was a good early childhood center, but she was not impressed when she came to observe and saw the morning activity: learning to dance to music of different tempos. "Don't you do anything educational?" she asked the teacher.

The teacher didn't know what to say. She had been taught that this kind of music and movement activity was good for children although she didn't really know why. She was "doing early childhood education" as she had been taught—the children loved it—but she didn't really know the reasons behind her own "developmentally appropriate practice."

Because this teacher didn't fully understand the reasons behind her early education practices, she couldn't explain the benefits of various classroom activities to either the parent or her new aide. And because she could not interpret her classroom to the parent, the parent was unlikely to view her classroom as an educational setting—a key reason why many parents see no justification for higher fees to pay staff higher wages. If she knew and could articulate the *why's* behind her practices, she might feel like a more professional teacher. She might also be able to promote her program and earn more professional wages.

This book was written to help just such a teacher answer parents' naïve yet unnerving questions about our classroom practices. This book explains *why* we do *what* we do in early care and education.

Knowing the why's behind our practices can also improve those practices. Many highly skilled early childhood teachers have developed an automatic and unconscious pattern of classroom practices. They don't have to think about what they are doing. But if this book makes them more conscious of their skills, of how these skills influence child development, then they can exercise those skills more consistently and teach them to new teachers more easily. Although Jean Piaget explained it better, Maria Montessori was the first to point out that people often learn unconsciously through everyday actions. But if we raise a skill to the conscious, conceptual level, then we have a new kind of control over that skill and can wield it in a more powerful way.

The ability to explain the why's of good practice is important for another reason. Policymakers are increasingly interested in expanding public education into lower age groups, beginning with a movement toward four-year-old kindergartens in many U.S. states. This trend could be very good, not only for young children, but also for elementary-aged children, because it could yield a partnership between early childhood and elementary education programs. Although there are many potential benefits to this relationship, there is also the chance that the methods common to elementary education might simply be extended downward into classrooms of four-year-olds and three-year-olds. This would be a disaster. In our view, elementary education may have more to learn from early care and education programs than the other way around.

Elementary teachers are trained in schools of education that often focus more on curriculum and the practice of teaching than on how children learn. If the teacher focuses on curriculum (the subject matter to be mastered), then providing the same instruction and experiences to the whole class at once seems natural and, indeed, efficient. And yet when the focus is on curriculum, treating a child's emotions may seem like a distraction from learning, rather than a key to motivating learning.

The roots of early childhood education lie more in the field of child psychology than education. Child psychology begins by asking how children grow and learn. When you're part of this tradition, teaching doesn't start with the curriculum, which places the emphasis on what children *don't* know. Instead, it begins with what the child currently knows and builds from there. In this approach, treating every child differently seems natural, as each child approaches a topic with different understandings and learns through her own experiences. Early childhood teachers and cognitive scientists understand knowledge in the same way: as something the child actively constructs through self-motivated action and experience, not as something poured into him.

We hope this book is useful not only to early childhood teachers, but also to the field of early care and education, because it shows the link between the practice of early childhood education and the science of child development. For example, petting the classroom bunny and talking about how the bunny feels may seem old-fashioned and "low tech";

it might look like mere play rather than education. And yet these are exactly the kind of activities scientists say we should be using to teach preschoolers important abilities such as perspective-taking, empathy, and prosocial behavior (see chapter 2). Similarly, playing Simon Says is fun, but it is also an exceptional method for teaching impulse control. Impulse control, which has been extensively studied by scientists, is considered an important early predictor of later success in school and in life (see chapter 3).

In the chapters that follow, we describe the science of child development and introduce corresponding information about classroom practices at appropriate points. Throughout the book you will find Practice Tips that offer practical guidance for working with young children based on scientific research. You will find vignettes in each chapter that highlight promising, as well as mistaken, practices based on notes we took observing early childhood programs. They show how scientific research on child development comes to life in real programs, with real people. Following chapters 1 through 3, you will find reproducible handouts you can give to parents explaining how the everyday practices in your program promote children's social-emotional development.

The two components of each chapter, one on science and one on practice, are really just two ways of talking about the same thing. Whatever aspect of child development we are discussing, highly professional practice comes from knowing both how children grow (the ages, stages, and processes of their development) and what we can do to promote that growth as early childhood teachers. You may read these parts independently or sequentially; the important thing to remember is that the two parts—science and practice—support and enrich each other. The science is meaningless unless we apply it, and the practices may be ineffective unless they are based on scientific research.

The linked fields of child development and early childhood education have much to teach each other as well as the broader field of education. We hope this book helps explain the scientific validity of early care and education practices, many of which look simpler than they are and have a much bigger impact on children's lives than may first appear.

A NOTE ON TERMS

Are you a child care provider? An early childhood teacher? Today these roles have merged, and everyone agrees that children grow best in settings that care for their physical, social, and emotional needs while stimulating their intellectual growth. To reflect both the caring and the educating components of helping young children grow, in this book we call the adult staff alternately "caregiver" and "teacher." We intend these terms to include everyone who works directly with young children. Whether you are a family child care provider or a kindergarten teacher, this book is for you.

1

Why We Hold a Crying Baby
Attachment and Exploration

Two-year-old Gina is visiting the early childhood program with her father. While he talks with Teacher Joan, Gina clings to his leg and looks around the room. Her gaze is drawn to three girls gluing leaves to headbands. She lets go of her father's leg and walks to their table. Suddenly a loud bang shoots across the room—a pot has fallen to the floor in the dramatic play area. Gina darts back to her father and pulls on him to pick her up. Other children pause, look to the source of the noise, and then look to the two teachers, who smile reassuringly. After two minutes of holding, Gina squirms to be put down and ventures out to resume her exploring.

What Is Attachment, and Why Is It Important?

Scenes like this play out daily in every corner of the world, because the behaviors of Gina and her father are part of our universal pattern of social development as humans. In particular, these behaviors show the workings of two of our *behavioral systems*, attachment and exploration. We know Gina has a secure attachment with her father because she uses him as a safe base from which to explore, and seeks comfort with him when scared. The other children in the room have formed attachments with the early childhood teachers and can calm themselves merely by looking across the room to make sure the teachers are still present. Simply put, *attachment* means a long-standing and emotionally strong tie between two people.

In this case the special bond is between young children and those who care for them.

Research on attachment has given us useful and unexpected information about relationships. Young children form strong attachments not only with their parents, but also with the other people who care for them consistently, including their early childhood teachers. These attachments can have a huge impact on children's futures. For example, children with secure attachments to one or more caregivers at twelve months of age are more compliant with adults as toddlers, get into fewer fights as preschoolers and grade-schoolers, and undergo greater intellectual development through the early childhood years. The attachment bonds children form with their first early childhood teachers also predict the quality of relationship they will have with future teachers, because this first relationship becomes the model for the others. We could reasonably argue that the most influential teacher in a child's life (after the parents), the one who has the largest overall impact on learning and success, is the child's first classroom teacher during early childhood.

SIGNS OF ATTACHMENT

To see whether a young child has become attached to you, look for these signs:

- ◆ the child looks at you and moves toward you following a separation.
- ◆ the child clings to you when upset and finds comfort in you.
- ◆ in your presence, the child feels safe enough to start looking around and exploring.

EARLY CHILDHOOD EDUCATION: A RELATIONSHIP-BASED JOB

We have all seen parents leaving their young child at an early childhood program for the first time, and we sense their feelings of discomfort. Leaving our "baby" with strangers, after all, goes against our instincts as humans. The parent might feel better if the early childhood teacher were a well-known member of the parent's family, such as a beloved aunt or brother. But on the first day of child care, the teacher is usually a stranger to both parent and child. Leaving their child in your care requires all the trust she has. Above all else, the parent must believe that you will love and protect his child as your own.

In all cultures, parents have always accepted the help of others, usually neighbors and family, in caring for their children. Today the early childhood teacher has been added to this group of helpers. At her best, she can function as a member of the extended family for both parent and child. This feeling of connectedness grants children security and can ease the uncertainty of parents who leave their child in your care.

How Attachment Affects Learning

For young children (and even adults at times), attachment and exploration represent opposing motivations and behaviors. Attachment comes from the desire to remain close to a caregiver and feel safe. Exploration comes from the desire to venture out and learn about the world. Children instinctively do both.

Children also instinctively create balance in their lives: when hungry they eat; when full they stop. Similarly, children create a balance between attachment and exploration. When a child decides to explore, we call this *secure base behavior*. The caregiver provides a secure base of physical and emotional safety, and the child maintains proximity to this base while exploring. The child ventures out but makes sure the caregiver remains within sight and sound. If something worries or frightens a child, he will use *approach behaviors* to move closer to the caregiver. This may include crawling toward the caregiver, raising her arms to be held, or whining to ask the caregiver to come closer. As children grow older, they venture further from their caregivers but still use this system of behaviors to maintain a balance between attachment and exploration. (Think about modern teenagers and the cell phone!)

The relationship between attachment and exploration can be seen both in and out of balance. For example, research studies find that most children play and explore much less when their caregiver leaves the room. This helps explain why children who are securely attached explore more and tend to learn more.[1] Feeling safe makes exploration possible. In fact, one team of researchers found that children with positive, secure attachments had better performance in tests of thinking skills through age seventeen.[2] By helping children feel cared for and safe, early childhood teachers prepare them to learn.

We can see the effect of attachment on exploration when children are new to an early care setting. In fact, even the way the child and parent separate for the day can make a difference. One research study observed how mothers prepared their two-year-olds for a brief separation. When mothers slipped out of the room without saying anything, their children played the least and were most likely to cry. In contrast, when mothers told their toddlers they were leaving and would return, or when they told their toddlers what they should do in the interim, their children played the most and cried the least.[3] Sneaking out might have been easier for the mothers, but it made the toddlers feel less safe. Thus, they did not explore or play as easily.

THE LINK TO LEARNING

Throughout the early childhood years, most learning depends on the formation of a nurturing relationship. For example, a child may be willing to look at the "scary lizards" only if you are there to hold his hand or even hold him on your hip. Another child may be afraid to join a game with other children, but having a caregiver stand by and watch may provide a secure enough base to join in. The learning of language, logic, and numbers is compromised if the child does not feel safe enough to explore and pay close attention. Above all else, the child must feel loved and safe.

Table 1.1 Bowlby's Stages in the Development of Attachment

Stage	Age range (months)	Child's behaviors
1. Pre-attachment	0–2	Indiscriminate responsiveness to different people
2. Attachment-in-the-making	2–7	Recognition of familiar people
3. Clear-cut attachment	7–24	Separation protest; increasing fear or wariness of strangers
4. Goal-corrected partnership	24 on	Understanding of caregivers' needs; more two-sided, mutual relationships

Source: Schaffer, H. R. 1996. *Social development*, 129. Oxford: Blackwell Publishers.

How Attachment Develops

Attachments that form between human babies and their caregivers differ from those found in most other mammals. Whereas geese and sheep *imprint* upon the first responsive object they see, and follow it around wherever it goes, human bonds form slowly over the first year of life.

In those earliest months, babies appear to quickly forget their parents or caregivers when they are not present. This forgetfulness is true of everything in their world. Babies think only of things immediately present. Furthermore, although they definitely prefer human company in these early months, they are not particular about who cares for them, as long as the caregiver is sensitive to their needs. We call this the period of *indiscriminate attachment*. You will often see this behavior when babies protest at being put down to sleep: it doesn't seem to matter who puts them down, they protest just the same.

Beginning around two or three months of age, infants can recognize familiar people when they reappear; we are rewarded with "social smiles" when they see us. But unless they can see or hear something, infants still seem unable to bring an image to mind. For them, the old saying is true: out of sight is out of mind. Over the first six months of life, babies slowly gain a mental picture of the particular people they can count on. At around six to eight months they develop *specific attachments* and respond to these people very differently than they respond to others.

THE ABILITY TO MISS SOMEONE

The development of specific attachments marks a milestone in children's reactions to separation from their parents. Early on, infants protest when a parent leaves the room, but the protest doesn't last long. Once they have formed a specific attachment and can remember the parent, their anxiety at separation grows much stronger and lasts longer. Infants begin to understand for the first time that objects (including people) exist even when they are not present. Pediatric nurses report that hospitalized babies under six months are relatively easy to settle and comfort when separated from their parents. But after about eight months calming and comforting become difficult. Child care workers see similar behavior with infants over seven months of age. When separated from their principal caregivers, for example, on their first day in a new setting, most infants will try to regain contact. If they fail, they will cry and protest, commonly for hours but possibly for many days. This is almost certainly because they continue to remember and miss their parents. Thus, starting child care before age six months, rather than after eight months, might be easier for both child and adult. Although untested by research, this makes sense intuitively.

PROMISING PRACTICE
Creating a New Relationship of Trust

What We Saw

Marcus is a seven-month-old infant, and this is his first day at the center. He cries through most of the morning, but Teacher Maria keeps him in her arms, often whispering his name and saying, "It's okay. I'm here." She sings to him in a low voice and holds him close. When we return to observe a week later, Marcus is crawling on a mat and watching other infants.

What It Means

Children need to feel secure before they can do anything else. Maria might have put the crying Marcus in a crib or high chair, but instead she did something much better: she made herself a reliable and comforting presence for him. Instead of serving her own needs (putting Marcus down), she served the child's needs. Over time, with a teacher who is dependably comforting, the child comes to view the teacher as a secure base for exploration. Anxieties are reduced; exploration and learning begin. Programs that strive for small group and low adult–child ratios support this best practice for teachers.

In this period of specific attachments, infants can form strong attachments to more than one person right from the start. Examples include both parents, an early childhood teacher, a grandparent, or an older sibling if any of them are consistent caregivers.[4] Young infants who used to smile at strangers gradually become wary or even fearful of them. Through these behaviors, children show that "people in general are not interchangeable and that attachment behavior has come to be focused on certain individuals only."[5]

We often think attachment issues occur only during the infant–toddler years. But as toddlers grow older, the desire to form relationships in which they feel safe and valued remains. Over time the relationships become more mature and adult-like. During the preschool years (starting around age two), many children become more independent and more cooperative in their relationships with adults. While young babies need to physically cling to their caregivers for comfort, preschoolers with positive attachments begin to internalize their trust, allowing them more independence. The trust they have developed with their primary caregivers helps them move into the stage of *goal-corrected partnerships*, in which the relationship between adult and child becomes less one-sided. The child starts to understand that caregivers have needs, too, and that the needs of both child and adult can be balanced. This growth in trust makes the morning separation much easier with preschoolers. They are more independent because they understand that parents need to work and they trust their parents will return for them later. The relationship between child and caregiver has become a partnership in which the goals of both are increasingly taken into account.

THE GIFT OF SECURE ATTACHMENT

"As you validate each child's essential goodness over and over during daily interactions, tuning in to their unique needs, you give the children in your care the priceless gift of secure attachment. This gift translates into more child courage, more competence, more friendliness, and the ability to rebound from life's troubles and empathize and cooperate with peers and adults—qualities every child care provider is eager for young children to achieve!"[6]

Differences in Early Attachments

Attachments differ not only in strength but also in type. Secure attachments are the most common type; however, there are two main types of insecure attachments, avoidant and resistant, each of which reflects very different kinds of parent–child behaviors.

The key to spotting a secure attachment is to watch the young child and caregiver when they reunite. In securely attached pairs, the child immediately goes to the caregiver, seeking and obtaining comfort. The caregiver is skilled at calming the child following the anxiety of separation.

Insecurely attached pairs are less skilled. Some infants or toddlers may look away from or even ignore the caregiver when they reunite (likely due to *anxious–avoidant attachment*). Others may go to the caregiver and reach up. But once picked up they refuse to be comforted, pushing the caregiver away (likely due to *anxious–resistant* attachment). In various ways, insecurely attached adult–child pairs are less successful at calming the child's anxiety and creating a safe base for exploration. While these infants or toddlers may be *strongly* attached, they are not *securely* attached.

How Can an Infant Be Strongly Yet Insecurely Attached?

Think of adult couples who are in constant conflict but who don't want to leave each other. For instance, a woman is battered by her boyfriend but refuses to leave him. Such a couple resembles anxiously attached children. The pair is strongly attached, but the attachment is insecure. In fact, researchers believe that an anxious pattern of attachment in early childhood is one predictor of problems in adult romantic relationships.[7]

If I Reward a Baby for Crying, Won't He Cry More?

Many parents and teachers worry about this. They think that if you attend to the baby every time she cries, it will just reward her for crying and teach her to cry more. When researchers studied this, however, they discovered the opposite: if you consistently meet a baby's needs—respond to his cries, for example—the baby cries less, not more.[8] This makes sense according to the attachment theories discussed above.

Babies instinctively cry when they have a need. Adults instinctively dislike that cry and want to do something about it. This is one of the ways nature ensures we do a good job of raising the next generation. The inborn desire to respond to a baby's cries is a good instinct to follow, as verified by research.

But Shouldn't I Teach the Child to Be More Independent?

Again, it may seem logical that we would help children become more independent by teaching them to calm themselves ("cutting the apron strings"). But research finds that during the first year, the exact opposite works better. Infants who have secure attachments—because their caregivers have consistently and sensitively responded to their needs—end up being the most independent toddlers and preschoolers.[9] The children who continue to have unmet needs are the ones who continue to cling to adults. The best way to create an independent child is to meet his needs and thus relieve the anxiety.

But Shouldn't I Teach the Child that I'm the Boss and the Child Can't Control Me by Crying?

Sorry, but babies don't think this way! Adults may think about control and power, but babies only react to their needs. A baby doesn't cry to make you feel bad; a baby cries because *she* feels bad (hungry, tired, wet, overstimulated, hot, etc.). Toddlers, however, are another matter. Their temper tantrums can really be a power struggle!

The Benefits of a Secure Attachment

About 70 percent of infants and toddlers have secure attachments with one or both of their parents. This is important for their current emotional health and future development. Researchers have followed children from infancy to adulthood[10] and find that having a secure attachment to at least one adult in the earliest years predicts better social relationships and better intellectual development in the years ahead. Several studies have found that having a secure attachment to an early childhood teacher enhances predictions for children's futures, even when they are securely attached to a parent.[11] But the greatest potential of early childhood programs is for those children who do not have a secure attachment with either parent. For them—roughly one in five—a secure relationship with a consistent caregiver in an early care and education program can open up new potentials for their development. In one study half of all children who lacked a secure attachment at home had a secure attachment with their child care teacher.[12]

Securely Attached Children Are More Compliant with Adults

Teaching children to comply with requests is an important goal for both parents and teachers. Research has shown that securely attached children tend to be more compliant as toddlers and preschoolers than insecurely attached children.[13] They are more compliant not only with their own parents, but also with other adults.

Even more interesting, securely attached toddlers appear to have greater "internalized control" of their behaviors; that is, they are learning to act appropriately on their own. This is important because our goal is not compliance with rules merely because we are watching them. The goal is greater self-control, over time, by internalizing rules (see chapter 3 on self-regulation). Researchers tested this capacity in toddlers by observing them in a room in which a fan was making a mobile spin.[14] They asked each child not to touch the fan or the mobile—which, of course, they all wanted to do. Securely attached children started reaching for the fan but *stopped themselves*, something the insecurely attached children couldn't do. (Of course, no child was ever allowed to touch the fan.)

Children in secure relationships may identify with their caregiver, want to be more like the caregiver, and have a greater desire to please their caregiver. For this reason, children are thought to be more open and accepting of their caregiver's requests because they have come to trust and value the caregiver. This mutual trust and caring are believed to help securely attached children merge their agenda with their caregiver's agenda so that everyone's needs can be met. For example, when a toddler whines for water in the supermarket, the father might say, "There is a drinking fountain at the end of this aisle; help me shop, and then we'll stop for water." A child with a secure attachment trusts this promise and is calmed, having learned that relationships are based on meeting each other's needs. A child at this stage is developing "goal-corrected partnerships" in which the goals of both child and adult are merged. In contrast, an insecurely attached child has learned that relationships cannot be trusted, and you are better off getting whatever you can, in any way, from another person.

Securely Attached Children Have Better Peer Relationships

Learning to get along with peers is one of the most important tasks of childhood (see chapter 2). The process begins very early in life, even before children can talk. It starts with children's emotional relationships with the adults who care for them. Children who experience secure attachment relationships have more success fitting in and getting along with others. They are more empathetic and make friends more easily. They are less likely to become bullies or victims of bullies.

For example, in one study researchers observed pairs of four-year-old friends playing.[15] The researchers had previously determined whether these children had secure or insecure attachments with their parents. When both members of the pair had secure attachments at home, they got along much better. They negotiated fairly and peacefully. On the other hand, if one member of the pair was insecurely attached, the interaction involved much more arguing and fighting.

Other researchers have looked specifically at the attachment bond between child care teachers and children. They found that this bond, too, predicts children's behavior both now and in the future. One of the most interesting series of studies found that four-year-olds who were securely attached to their current teacher engaged in more complex play, were friendlier, and were less aggressive with peers in the child care setting.[16] It was no surprise that securely attached toddlers were more socially competent with peers. But researchers were surprised to find that children's infant teachers, from three years earlier, also had a significant effect on social competence at age four. Attachment with the preschool teacher matters, but so does the child's earlier attachment with his first caregiver during infancy. A later follow-up with these same children at age nine showed that having a secure attachment with their very first early childhood teachers was a strong predictor of positive relationships with their elementary school teachers and peers.[17]

SPOTTING TYPES OF ATTACHMENT IN THE CLASSROOM

The type of attachment that young children have with their child care teachers can be observed in their behaviors.[18]

Securely attached children:

- accept comfort when they are upset.
- can usually be calmed by the teacher holding them.
- spontaneously hug the teacher.
- easily follow her directions.
- are lighthearted and playful with the teacher.

Insecure/avoidant attached children:

- are more interested in the materials in the classroom than in the teacher or the other children.
- act as if they do not hear what the teacher says or notice what he does.
- avoid frequent or close contact with the teacher.
- do not seek comfort from the teacher when hurt or upset, and might even move away from the teacher if she moves closer to comfort them.

Insecure/resistant (ambivalent) attached children:

- resist classroom routines such as cleaning up.
- are demanding and impatient with the teacher and are not satisfied with his attempts to respond.
- cry to get the teacher to do what they want her to do.
- cling when the primary teacher attempts to leave the room and continue to cry after he leaves.

WORKING WITH AN INSECURELY ATTACHED CHILD

Children who have insecure attachments with their parents will bring that same relationship style to their interactions with you. They will be less competent at using you, the teacher, to calm themselves or to support their efforts at self-control. This is no fun for the child, and having an undercontrolled child is certainly no fun for you! What can you do?

- Keep working, consistently and persistently, on your own relationship with the child.
- Be reliably sensitive and responsive.

Over a period of one to several months, the child can form a different kind of attachment with you, based on trust. You will become increasingly able to calm her simply by your presence, by making eye contact, or by speaking gently. You will have given her a wonderful advantage for the future: a model of how to interact competently with a teacher.

As noted above, secure attachments in early childhood influence the quality of children's relationships for years to come. One research team followed a group of children from birth to adolescence.[19] They assessed security of attachment in infancy and then asked parents and teachers to rate how well these children got along with others throughout childhood and adolescence. Of all the factors considered, the best predictor of success with peers in the teenage years was the quality of their attachment as one-year-olds! From their earliest interactions with their main caregivers, these children had learned how to create a mutually satisfying relationship with others.

When infants and toddlers with secure attachments grow into teenagers and adults, they tend to select romantic partners who, like themselves, view relationships based on mutuality, combining agendas, and meeting each other's needs.[20] In contrast, people who learn the lessons of insecure attachments have less stable intimate relationships and tend to view them selfishly: what can I get from the other person?

Table 1.2 Strategies to Ease the Transition into Child Care

WITH YOUNG AND MOBILE INFANTS

Strategy	Why it helps
On the first visit, encourage the parent to hold the infant (or leave her in the car seat).	Gives the child some distance and time to adjust to you.
Hold the child gently, facing outward.	The child can focus on the environment and may forget that you are a stranger.
Assign a primary caregiver.	Builds a bond of trust and predictability. The child feels more control.
Make mildly silly faces and look for the child's reaction.	Engages the child's attention in a nonthreatening way.
Talk soothingly and sing to the child.	Calms the child and builds a bond.
Hold the child in your lap, and read books to him.	Engages the child's attention.
Dance with the infant.	Rhythmic movement is soothing and builds a bond.

WITH TODDLERS AND PRESCHOOLERS

Strategy	Why it helps
Establish a good-bye ritual that the parent, child, and teacher follow each day. For example, upon arrival, the child hangs up his coat and greets the teacher. Together they walk the parent to the door and wave good-bye out the window.	A familiar routine provides predictability; the child has an active role, and some control, in the situation.
Tell the child before the parent leaves: "Daddy's going to work now, and he'll be back later to pick you up."	Builds predictability and trust, and therefore security.
Talk about the child's feelings: "You're sad that Mommy had to go, but she'll be back after naptime."	The child feels understood, thus building trust.
Have a blanket, stuffed animal, pacifier, or other "security" object on hand.	Transitional objects create a feeling of security so the child can be more independent. They are called transitional objects because they help the child make the transition from complete dependence upon caregivers to eventual independence.
Introduce a buddy.	Having a familiar friend calms the child and may distract her from the anxiety of separation.
Give the child a favorite toy.	Anything familiar is calming. Having a familiar toy the child can play with creates predictability while attracting the child's attention and engagement.
Provide a new toy.	New toys attract the child's attention and encourage him to explore.
Post photos of the child's family where the child can see them.	Connects the child to home and family, and creates continuity.
Maintain a consistent teacher presence.	Builds a bond of trust and predictability; the child feels more in control.

WITH PARENTS

Strategy	Why it helps
Meet with the parent before the child begins the program to go over child's schedule, preferences, routines, etc.	Gives you key information to care for the child, while establishing positive communication and building trust in the parent.
Allow time for the transition between home and school. Encourage visits to the program before the first day. Begin the first few days with a limited stay, or invite the parent to stay for a portion of them.	Gives the child and parent time to get comfortable and build trust in the new setting and its new people.
Create a good-bye ritual (read a book or play with a toy before leaving, walk to the door together, use the same kind of good-bye each day, etc.).	Gives a sense of control and predictability to the parent as well as the child.
Pass young children from parent to teacher—an important part of the ritual.	Symbolizes the transfer of responsibility for the child; over time, it comes to symbolize the parent's trust.
Announce the parent's departure.	Supports the parent in leaving while providing predictability for the child.
Ask the parent to bring pictures of the child's family and home for mounting on the wall or in the classroom book.	Creates a feeling of continuity between home and school for parent as well as child. It tells the parent that her whole family matters to this early care and education program, not just the child.
Give the parent daily schedules and/or lesson plans, as well as daily reports of the child's experiences. Ask the parent about the child's daily or nightly issues.	Helps the parent feel more connected to his child's day, less separated from his child, and more in partnership with the teacher.
Send a "first-day" fax or e-mail to the parent.	Parent feels less separated from her child and more in partnership with the teacher. Builds trust.
Have an open door policy that allows parents to visit, check in, or volunteer anytime they like.	Parent feels welcomed, building trust more quickly as you show that your program clearly has nothing to hide.
Use a warm, calm, and matter-of-fact approach that says "everything will be okay."	Parent and child will take your cue that everything is okay. Confidence will grow.

Why Early Attachments Matter

Long before children learn to speak, they learn core lessons about themselves through their attachment relationships. They carry these lessons into the world as assumptions about the world and their place in it.

1. *Children learn that their caregiver will be available in times of need.* Attachment relationships help children feel safe and secure. Children learn that they can trust their caregiver; if needed, he will be there to help or comfort. They learn confidence in social relationships.

2. *Children learn that they deserve the loving attention they receive.* From infancy through preschool, consistent attention from a caregiver teaches children that their wants and needs are important. From these regular messages children learn that they are special people, worthy of love and attention. They learn self-confidence.

3. *Children learn what to expect from social relationships.* Researchers call these expectations "internal working models."[21] They influence how children think about and create their future relationships with others. For example, a child who has good experiences with her caregiver will expect similar experiences in other social relationships. In other words, children fit their future relationships into the molds of their past relationships.

4. *Children learn how to interact appropriately with others.* By around six weeks of age infants already show a clear preference for human social contact,[22] and their early exchanges with adults begin to teach them how to interact with other people. Infants' interactions with caregivers help them learn:

   - how to get another person's attention.
   - how to focus attention on a person's face.
   - how to take turns when interacting with others.

As children grow, their interactions with caregivers become more complex.[23]

Toddlers' interactions with caregivers and preschool-aged children help them learn:

- how to share and compromise.
- how to communicate.
- how to cope with negative emotions.

Depending on their early experiences with adult caregivers, children come to have very different views of the world and their place in it ("internal working models"). These views are summarized in Table 1.3.

Table 1.3 Attachments Lead to Core Beliefs

	Securely attached	Insecurely attached
View of self	I am worthy of love.	I am not worthy.
View of others	Other people are fun.	Other people cannot be trusted.
View of relationships	I care for others. I take turns and compromise.	I manipulate others to get what I want.

A HUMAN RELATIONSHIP PROFESSION

The job of the early childhood teacher has much in common with other human relations jobs, such as therapist or counselor. The goal of your work is to promote other people's emotional health, and your most powerful tool is the relationship you build. Everything else you do with young children shrinks in importance compared to the relationship you form with them.

This idea goes back a long way in the field of early childhood. It was central to the education textbooks of a half century ago, such as Katherine Read's classic text, *The Nursery School: A Human Relations Laboratory* (1950). According to Read, the emotional health of the teacher herself is a key influence in the education of young children. The more self-aware and emotionally healthy the teacher, the more effective she is at guiding and teaching young children. In this, Read was echoing the view of contemporary psychotherapy researchers who had also noted that successful therapy depends upon the emotional health of the therapist.

According to Alice Sterling Honig, one of Read's successors, "You can respond with maturity and calm only when you are in tune with your own feelings."[24] Honig recommended cultivating supportive, caring friendships with people who can help you reflect on your own past and present relationships. Only with a clear understanding of your own life and relationships can you achieve enough emotional clarity to create healthy relationships with the children in your care. According to Honig, this is something every early childhood teacher can work on.

We could say without exaggeration that the practice of early childhood education is, at its best, a form of preventive psychotherapy!

It is a fact that children's relationships with infant and preschool caregivers have long-term effects. The explanation lies in brain development. A number of studies have now confirmed what psychologists predicted: the patterns of early attachment shape the developing brain.[25] While these patterns can be changed at any age, it is difficult because the physical structures of the brain resist change.

ATTACHMENT WITH CULTURAL SENSITIVITY IN MIND

Imagine how unsettling it would be for a young child to be left in the care of a teacher who looks very different from her family, is of a different race, or speaks a different language. Perhaps, too, the way the other children are playing is different from the children's play in her culture. Keep in mind that the rules of a child care program may make sense in one culture and not in another. For example, in the parents' culture a child carrying transitional objects (an old stuffed animal or a tattered security blanket) might seem perfectly normal, while the teacher might frown and want the child to be more independent.

Talking with parents to find out their family and cultural beliefs will help you build routines with the children that are consistent with their home routines, especially with respect to daily events such as lunch and nap. Adopting these routines at the outset can help the child feel comfortable with you. For example, an infant is used to being held in a certain position for feeding or burping; a toddler is used to being read a favorite book before naptime.

Attachment is a universal aspect of child development, and children from all cultures benefit from having a secure attachment relationship. However, the exact ways in which caregivers are sensitive to and respond to the child may differ from one culture to another, from one family to another, or from one teacher to another. With careful observation and respectful conversations, we can learn how other cultures promote secure attachment. We don't need to agree with parents at all times or do everything just as they do, but as their partners we should be ready to discuss and respect cultural differences.

How Teachers Can Support Secure Attachments

While the development of attachment between caregiver and child is based partly on instinct, it isn't automatic. The first social bonds are created as the caregiver gradually learns to read the child and respond sensitively. Caregivers who know how to read children ask themselves, "What is this child thinking/feeling now?" or "What is this child trying to tell me by acting this way?" At the same time, the child gradually learns about the caregiver, including how to regulate the caregiver's behavior: how to bring the caregiver closer or how to enlist the caregiver's soothing voice and touch. Researchers have found much supporting evidence for this mutual learning process.[26]

One study of securely attached children and their caregivers highlights how caregivers create secure attachments. From the children's first months, these caregivers were highly consistent and sensitive in response to the infants in their care. They were warm and nurturing in predictable ways. They had more skill establishing the right pace during interactions and more skill using routines. They were more responsive to babies' cries. As a result, the infants in their care came to cry less than other infants.[27] In fact, over time, these caregivers could sometimes calm their infants from across the room just by talking to them. Caregiver–infant pairs such as these create a well-functioning team: the baby is effective at communicating with the caregiver and the caregiver is effective at understanding and meeting the baby's needs. Looking at this data, researchers believe that infants such as these come to see the world as a trustworthy place, where their needs will be met. This core belief, along with the skill of the caregiver, makes the child easier to comfort over time.[28]

In contrast, children with insecure attachments to both parents, who make up about 20 percent of all infants and toddlers, are often unsure what to expect from their caregivers. Sometimes the caregiver is available and nurturing, sometimes not. Sometimes the caregiver is unresponsive. Sometimes the caregiver might even be scary.

Practice Tip

Creating Secure Attachments in Early Childhood Settings

- Use multiage groupings of children, so a child can stay with the same teacher for multiple years. This practice also allows older and younger siblings to remain together, which can make the transition to child care much easier for younger children.

- Try "looping," in which the teacher moves with the children from the infant room to the toddler room and even up to the preschool room. Continuity in relationships can also be achieved by keeping the teacher and children in the same room as they age, adapting the room to meet changing developmental needs.

- Organize work schedules and assignments within multiteacher rooms so that there are smaller "attachment groups" in which each teacher provides consistent care for only a small number of children. The teacher in this situation is often called the "primary caregiver" of his small group.

- At the beginning of the day, have the parent drop off the child with a teacher who knows her well, rather than with a part-time teacher or in a drop-off room.

- At the end of the day, try to have the parent pick up his child from a teacher who is well aware of how the child's day went.

PROBLEMATIC PRACTICES

The economics of early care and education makes attachment-based practices difficult. Here are some examples:

- To make child care more affordable, many programs raise their adult–child ratios and group sizes, but this makes the development of teacher–child attachment bonds more difficult.

◆ Children in some programs are moved from room to room during the day to maintain the adult–child ratios required by licensing regulations.

◆ Annual staff turnover rates average 30 to 40 percent,[29] which means that a child who develops an attachment to a caregiver often suffers the loss of that relationship. On the other hand, some observers believe that when early childhood teachers adopt practices that strengthen teacher–child attachments, teachers are less likely to leave midyear, to avoid the emotional loss.[30]

How do teachers support the formation of secure attachments? Just like the evidence on parents, teachers who are more sensitive in their interactions with young children are more likely to form secure attachment relationships with them. Research also shows that secure attachment is more likely in classrooms with fewer children per adult. This makes sense. With fewer children, the teacher has more time for each child and can be more consistent and reliable in answering each child's call for help or need for love.[31]

Two other factors can influence whether a child will form a secure attachment with his teacher: the amount of time spent with the teacher and the number of primary teachers the child has.[32] This helps explain why, in one study, researchers found that distressed children were much more likely to seek comfort from senior staff than from new staff, and that senior staff were more successful at soothing their distress.[33] The longer and more stable the relationship between caregiver and child is, the more likely they will share a secure attachment.[34]

✔️ Practice Tips with Infants and Toddlers

Believe in the Value of Spending Time Connecting with Each Child

- Slow down when doing routine caregiving activities such as diapering and feeding.
- Talk to the child about what you are doing.
- Even with infants, try to establish a routine of taking turns. After you say something to the infant, pause and wait for a response (perhaps a gurgle or wiggle). Then say something or tickle the infant again, and wait for a response. Learning to take turns is fundamental to human relationships, and the process helps the infant feel connected to you.
- Respond promptly to the young child's distress signals.
- Use words to describe what children are experiencing. Give them language for their feelings and thoughts.
- Give the child lots of physical contact by holding, carrying, rocking, and massaging.
- Allow transitional objects (security blanket or favorite stuffed animal) if not during the whole day, then during key parts of the day (such as naptime). There is no harm in them, and they help children feel more secure and become more independent of adult caregivers. Children will stop using them when they feel more secure and when peers begin making fun of them.

PROMISING PRACTICE

Managing Separation Anxiety

What We Saw

Elaine is a fairly new four-year-old in the center. Arriving in the morning, she holds her father's leg and resists taking off her coat. Teacher Tim gets down on one knee and holds out his hands to her. She goes to him but begins to cry. Tim nods to the father and says to Elaine, "I know you are sad, but Dad has to leave. He will be back to pick you up later." As the father leaves, teacher and child wave to him. Teacher Tim and Elaine sit near two other girls playing with blocks. Within a minute, Elaine climbs down from Tim's lap to join in the play. Tim gets up and moves to a different group of children.

What It Means

Separation anxiety reaches a peak at age one, but as with Elaine, it can continue long after. Building trust with a new teacher and a new environment takes time. Tim's sensitivity toward Elaine and her father helps. Tim gives her physical comfort and finds a fun activity to engage her. Once she's engaged, he can move on. A difficult, emotional transition was handled skillfully in just a few minutes' time.

Can Attachment Change?

When a child's family situation is stable, the security or insecurity of her attachments also tends to stay stable over time. But when a child's family situation changes, her attachment relationships are open to change as well. For example, when a parent starts a new job, loses a job, gets married, or divorces, or when the household moves or another baby is born, the attachment bond between child and caregiver can change. Sometimes it changes for the better, sometimes for the worse. Young children who live in unsettled circumstances have attachments that more often change between secure and insecure.[35]

But even if the parent–child attachment doesn't improve, the early childhood teacher can form an attachment that can make all the difference to the child. For example, one study found that children who had a secure attachment with their mothers as well as with their child care teachers were more socially skilled than those with a secure attachment to just one caregiver.[36]

 *Practice Tip*

Separation Distress

Separations are difficult for young children and often for their parents too. Children younger than eight months of age experience little separation distress. After that, it rises rapidly in both incidence and intensity to a peak at about twelve months. Then it slowly drops over the next few years.[37]

Parents may think it's easier for their child if they slip away unnoticed while their child is distracted. (They may find it easier on themselves, too, because they avoid seeing their child's distress.) However, a parent's unexpected disappearance can make matters much worse for the child than an acknowledged departure. Reassure parents that the distress caused by their departure is normal for children starting a child care program. Encourage them to establish a good-bye routine, saying and doing exactly the same things at each separation. Routines create predictability and reassure the child that parents who leave also come back! If a parent needs guidance, teach him. (Parents may need your help as much as the child.) You can tell him to say: "I'm leaving now. I love you very much and will be back later to pick you up, just like I do every day. Give me a big hug." Here are some other tips:

- ◆ Suggest to parents that they visit the child care program with their child a few times before the first full day. Experiment with very brief separations.
- ◆ Starting at about ten months of age, some programs give the child a photo of the parent(s) and child together. It is placed where the child can get it and carry it around, if desired. It's a tangible reminder of the parent–child bond that helps ward off anxiety about the separation.[38]
- ◆ Instruct parents to avoid revealing their own distress and act in a loving but businesslike manner. While separations are hard for them, too, the child will become more upset if they show it. Through their behavior, parents need to communicate, "This is normal and okay."

How Early Child Care Affects Attachments Between Parent and Child

Researchers in the 1980s began to worry that early, full-time child care could harm the security of attachment. Five studies found that infants placed in full-time child care in their first year were about 20 percent less likely to have secure attachments with their parents, a finding that alarmed some scholars. It can be explained in part by the theory of attachment. If the infant interpreted the parent's absence during the day at child care as rejection or lack of reliable availability, then this 20 percent shift of children from secure to insecure attachment made perfect sense. These scholars warned parents against using full-time child care with infants during their first year of life.[39] Other scholars wondered whether the daily separation was the problem or whether it might be something else, such as frequent changes of child care or lower-quality child care.

WHAT DOES IT MEAN WHEN A TODDLER CALLS HER TEACHER "MOMMY"?

If the mother hears it, she is usually filled with jealousy, anger, and guilt. She may wonder whether she is doing the right thing by placing her child in child care or whether it makes her a bad mom who has now been replaced by the child care teacher.

Early childhood teachers may also have mixed feelings when called "Mommy" or "Daddy." Embarrassment precedes a bit of pride and pleasure. Good early childhood teachers *love* the children in their care and feel good when that love is reciprocated. But they may feel guilty as well, if they believe they are taking the parent's place.

The good news is that, according to the best available research, the teacher does not replace the parent.[40] Even better news: from the child's point of view, none of this is a problem at all. Children need an attachment to a sensitive and reliable adult in each of their major settings. Calling the early childhood teacher "Mommy" is actually a very good sign. "Mommy" is the child's word for anyone who is reliably nurturing (just as some children call every four-legged animal "doggy"). Child care teachers must understand how important it is to explain this carefully to the mother!

This was such an important controversy that the main researchers on both sides of the question got together and formed a single research team. After following a large group of children from the time they were born, the researchers found that child care experiences alone did not threaten the quality of parent–child attachments. The strongest predictor of the child's attachment to her parents was the parents' own sensitivity to their child. But child care was significant for the mother–child bond. If the mother's sensitivity and responsiveness were low, then the mother–child attachment was especially likely to be insecure when combined with low-quality child care, multiple care arrangements, or extensive hours in child care.[41]

In other words, the quality of child care is much more important for the child who has an insecure attachment to her mother. This is consistent with a common theme in many research studies: the child at risk—through poverty, parental insensitivity, a learning disability, or any other way—is the child for whom the early childhood setting can make the biggest difference.

Can Children Become More Attached to the Child Care Provider Than to Their Parents?

Parents can also have mixed feelings when their child forms a warm bond with the early childhood teacher. When their toddler hugs the teacher's knee and refuses to go home at the end of the day, parents may worry that they are being replaced in their child's affections. After all, when a parent works full time, his child may spend as many waking hours with the teacher as with the parent.

Researchers, too, wondered whether parents were being replaced.[42] In one experiment, an infant or toddler from a full-day, full-week child care program was placed in the middle of a room with a toy that made loud noises. Mother was on one side of the room, early childhood teacher on the other. Both adults were instructed not to talk or gesture to the child. To whom would the child go when distressed by the loud noise?

THE CRUCIAL VALUE OF ONE GOOD RELATIONSHIP

The scientist Urie Bronfenbrenner had a fun yet accurate way to summarize the importance of attachment. He wrote that "in order to develop normally, a child needs the enduring, irrational involvement of one or more adults. . . . In short, somebody has to be crazy about the kid."[43] The very best care and education is almost certainly provided by adults who have fallen in love with the children in their care. They are crazy about their kids!

The results showed that children moved closer to their mothers more often than to their teachers. (Children moved closer to their teachers, however, when the other choice was a stranger.) The same pattern held true when the experiment involved sharing toys, communicating, and extent of physical contact. Although it is fair to assume that many of these children were securely attached to their teachers, teachers did not replace mothers.

Such studies support the view that child care teachers do not compete with parents. In fact, just the opposite is true: teachers support parents in providing the most stimulating and nurturing childhoods possible. The closer and more secure the child's attachment to the teacher is, the better the child's development is.

Further Reading

On Research

Colin, V. L. 1996. *Human attachment*. New York: McGraw-Hill.

On Practice

Edwards, C. P., and Raikes, H. 2002. Extending the dance: Relationship-based approaches to infant–toddler care and education. *Young Children* 57 (4):10–17.

Gonzalez-Mena, J. 2005. Attachment and separation. In *Diversity in early care and education: Honoring differences*, 4th ed., edited by J. Gonzalez-Mena, 79–91. New York: McGraw-Hill.

Honig, A. S. 2002. *Secure relationships: Nurturing infant/toddler attachment in early care settings.* Washington, D.C.: National Association for the Education of Young Children.

Howes, C., and Ritchie, S. 2002. *A matter of trust: Connecting teachers and learners in the early childhood classroom.* New York: Teachers College Press.

Hyson, M. 2004. *Emotional development of young children: Building an emotion-centered curriculum*, 2nd ed. New York: Teacher's College Press.

Children's Books

Brown, M. W. 1972. *The runaway bunny*. New York: Harper & Row.

Henkes, K. 2000. *Wemberly worried*. New York: Greenwillow Books.

Joosse, B. M. 1991. *Mama, do you love me?* San Francisco: Chronicle.

Kern, N. 1998. *I love you with all my heart*. San Francisco: Chronicle.

McCourt, L. 1997. *I love you, stinky face*. Minneapolis: Bridgewater Books.

Munsch, R. 1986. *Love you forever*. Ontario: Firefly.

Smith, W. 2001. *Just the two of us*. New York: Scholastic Press.

Viorst, J. 1992. *The good-bye book*. New York: Alladin Books.

Weeks, S. 2002. *My somebody special*. New York: Gulliver Books.

Williams, V. B. 1990. *More more more*. New York: Greenwillow Books.

~~~~~~

When Teachers Reflect: *Teachers Feel Loss Too*

- Early research on attachment looked at infants' feelings of emotional loss when separated from their primary caregivers and found it to be authentic.[44] For example, children can really miss their former early childhood teachers when parents move them from one child care arrangement to another or when a child care center moves a child to a different room and teacher. But you may ask yourself: what about the teacher? What does a teacher feel when a child with whom she has formed an attachment is removed? What can early care and education programs do to minimize such loss in the lives of both teachers and children?

~~~~~~

When Teachers Reflect: *The Hard-to-Love Children*

Some children are harder to love than others. They are neither as easy nor as rewarding to work with. They resist cuddling by going limp in your arms; they may even hit you or push you away. Because they are less capable of attracting the kind of adult attention they need, they probably need your caring even more. Their habits of thinking and behaving will make it more difficult to make positive changes in the future. Now, while they are young, is the easiest and most effective time to teach these hard-to-love children about relationships. Here are some steps you can take to promote attachment with them:

- Use a slower and more cautious approach. Cuddling that feels good to other children may feel intrusive or even scary to them. Gain their trust slowly and deliberately over time. Use sensitive, consistent interactions and rituals to build predictability into your relationship. Predictability is the beginning of trust.
- Think of a child you know who goes limp in your arms, pushes you away, is harder to love. How can you change your greetings, routines, and interactions with him (and the parents) to build trust and social competence?

~~~~~~

Letter to Parents

Children often miss their parents when they are young. We believe that if we work as partners, we can all make sure every child feels welcomed, secure, and loved in our early childhood program.

Did You Know?

When young children feel safer and more loved, they actually learn more. Until children feel safe here, they will not explore the materials or learn as much from our activities. In fact, research studies have found that having a warm, secure relationship with an adult in the early childhood program predicts better performance in thinking skills, right through childhood and into the teenage years.

Did You Know?

When children have a warm and secure relationship with their early childhood teacher, they get along better with other children in the current year and for years to come.

Did You Know?

When children have a warm and secure relationship with their earliest teacher, they are much more likely to feel that way about their other teachers later, even their elementary school teachers.

Research studies have confirmed what we knew intuitively: the emotional well-being of children makes a big difference in how they succeed in our early childhood program today and in later schooling too.

We are dedicated to a partnership with you, the parents, to provide the best possible care and early education for your child. Let us know how we are doing and how we can do better.

From *Social and Emotional Development: Connecting Science and Practice in Early Childhood Settings* (Redleaf Press, 2007).

2

Why We Talk about How the Bunny Feels
Friendship and Prosocial Behavior

Alex has a lot of fun with his friends in the child care setting. Although he spends most of his time with two friends, he gets along with most of the other children too. All the teachers agree that Alex is thriving in their early care and education program. In contrast, Caleb has no consistent playmates. He makes attempts to join in different activities sometimes, but he does not often succeed. The staff is looking for ways to help Caleb make friends and become more involved in the class.

In the last chapter we considered the importance of children's earliest relationships with the adults who care for them. In this chapter we consider another relationship: the friendship or peer relationship between two children. As in the last chapter, we see that early relationships can have a big impact on children's futures, and once again, child care teachers can play a key role in starting a child on the right path.

Why Peer Relationships Matter

We hope that young children make friends in their early care and education setting because we want them to feel welcome and included. Friendship is one of life's joys. Encouraging friendship, as good child care teachers do, promotes children's long-term development. The quality of peer relationships in early childhood predicts later success in intellectual growth, self-esteem, mental health, and school performance.[45] Researchers who followed a group of children throughout childhood and into adolescence found that those who got along well with peers during the preschool years continued to do so during adolescence.[46] In contrast, children who had difficulties with peer relationships during this time continued to have difficulties as they got older. Of course, these results do not mean that a child's social life is fully determined at an early age. But unless we do something to change their paths, they tend to continue down those built in their preschool years.

Although most studies on the impact of early peer relationships on later life outcomes looked at the early elementary years rather than the preschool years, the results are compelling. A number of studies found that unpopular children do not perform as well in school[47] and are more likely to drop out of school in adolescence.[48] They are also more likely to get into legal trouble.[49] Some studies that followed young children into adulthood found that socially isolated children were more likely than others to have bad-conduct discharges from military service[50] and emotional or mental health problems as adults.[51] Considering the results of these studies, children's peer relationships begin to look like more than just fun. In fact, they are a critical indicator of future success in life.

What makes these early peer relationships so important for children's future development? How well they get along with peers—the quality of their interactions—affects how much children learn. Since children spend much of their daily lives interacting with peers, a big part of their learning and development occurs within these relationships. In the extreme case, children who are rejected or ignored by others may develop problems in personal adjustment, social skills, and learning. Of course, adults influence children's development in these areas too. But relationships with peers have some features that differ from adult–child relationships and may create unique opportunities for development.

PROMISING PRACTICE

A Game That Requires Prosocial Behavior

What We Saw

The teachers brought out a large colorful parachute. Four adults placed themselves in key spots around the parachute, and about a dozen children joined in holding its handles. A ball was placed in the middle, and everyone had to work together to launch it into the air. The teacher asked, "Did you get it up high or low?" The children yelled out, "High!" The next time the ball didn't go very high, and the teacher said, "It went low because we didn't work together. Let's try again. Ready, 1–2–3!" Everyone worked together, and the ball went high into the air. The children yelled, "We did it! We did it!"

What It Means

This game requires children to pay attention to each other and work together. It's like being on a teeter-totter: it just doesn't work unless you cooperate! The game itself guides and rewards children for learning to pay attention to others.

PROMISING PRACTICE

Promoting Prosocial Interactions with Toddlers

What We Saw

The teacher is helping Elaine build a tower of blocks. When Anjuli comes over, Elaine slaps her away. The teacher says to Elaine, "Nice . . . that's your friend." Elaine points to the other child, and the teacher says, "Anjuli." The children continue pointing to each other, and the teacher repeats their names.

What It Means

The teacher is promoting prosocial behavior. She responds to Elaine's aggressive behavior with a reminder that describes the positive behavior she wants the child to use. This is teaching. She then responds to Elaine's pointing by giving her the name of the person Elaine pointed to. Toddlers frequently use "point and name" to interact with adults. Here, the teacher's naming of each child reinforces their connection to one another. Elaine and Anjuli enjoy a pleasant activity together, but only with the teacher's assistance.

What's Different about Peer Relationships?

Unlike their relationships with adults, children's peer relationships are interactions between equals. Physically, emotionally, socially, and intellectually, peers are on a level playing field. For this reason, they offer a type of learning experience different from adult relationships. Adults teach children and guide their emerging abilities. In contrast, peer interactions let children practice and refine what they have learned from their adult teachers. For example, children practice their language skills during conversations with peers. They also learn about fairness and negotiation with peers, because negotiation works best between equals.

The unique features of peer relationships help explain why they play such an important role in children's development. However, peer relationships can be very challenging to many toddlers and preschoolers. Since many children make their first same-age friends in the early care and education setting, guiding their earliest encounters becomes an important role of early childhood professionals. But before reviewing the research on the teacher's role, we will review the research on early peer interactions.

How Peer Relationships Develop

A child's tendency to engage others socially and to seek attention or approval is called *sociability*.[52] In some ways, infants are inherently social. They prefer human voices to other sounds. Because human newborns are so dependent on other humans for their survival, this orientation toward other humans is adaptive. By six weeks, infants prefer the company of people to nonsocial stimulation. Within the first three months they begin to smile and coo, and attempt to gain the attention of people. By three months, most babies get excited when they see someone they know (giving "social smiles"); soon after, they may start showing shyness or fear around strangers.

Some of the first signs of peer interaction occur around three to four months of age when infants show interest in other infants and sometimes reach out to touch them. By six months, children begin to smile at, and gesture toward, one another, perhaps even offering toys. During the second half of the infant's first year, social behaviors become more frequent. Some infants may point out toys to peers (a remarkably young attempt to create "joint attention") and imitate behavior. It may be infrequent and inconsistent, but even infants are aware of and react to peers.

After age one, children increase their peer activities. Toddlers make more deliberate attempts to gain peers' attention, to get them to respond in some way. By eighteen months, behavior toward peers is more consistently social. Smiling and imitation, as responses, are much more frequent. Their enjoyment is clear. By twenty-four months, their interaction really begins to look like play. For example, they are playing when they chase each other and when they help each other pull out toys.

Although children continue to enjoy the attention of adults, their preference for, and sophistication with, peers increases each year. Researchers in one study followed a group of children from infancy through age five and showed how peer interactions develop over time. Table 2.1 lists the types of play observed, from the simple (in which infants merely acknowledge each other) to the complex (in which preschoolers carry out elaborate role plays), and the age at which they typically emerge.[53]

Table 2.1 Children's Peer Play Develops Gradually

Typical age when behavior first appears	Type of Play	Example
6–12 months	Parallel play—two children perform similar activities without acknowledging each other.	Two infants sit next to each other playing with "busy boxes." They do not notice each other's activities.
6–12 months	Parallel aware play—parallel play with eye contact.	Infants notice each other as they play independently.
12–18 months	Simple social play—similar activities while interacting.	Two children play with stuffed animals. They smile at one another and exchange animals.
18–24 months	Complementary and reciprocal play—children demonstrate action-based role reversals in social games.	Two children play run-and-chase or peekaboo.
2–3 years	Cooperative social pretend play—role-playing without any planning or negotiating about the meaning of the roles or how the play will progress.	A child makes a "bus" using blocks. The child gets on the "bus" and starts to drive. Another child gets on the bus as a "passenger."
3–4 years	Complex social pretend play—planned role-playing: children assign each other roles; a "script" is proposed and changed if necessary.	Two children plan a "birthday party." One child says that she will be the mom and the second child will be the son. The second child then suggests that they have cake at the party.

Peer relationships, of course, go beyond mere sociability and interaction skills. Some become more important than others, and preferred playmates evolve. In this way, children's earliest friendships develop over time.

The Benefits of Early Friendships

Infants and young toddlers often have preferred playmates, and three- to four-year-olds display clear preferences that indicate a friendship bond.[54] In other words, even preschool-aged children have real friendships. Compared to those of peers who are not friends, the interactions of preschool-aged friends are much more complex and coordinated.[55] Preschool-aged friends appear happier during their interactions and are better at dealing with conflict than nonfriends. Young children are also more skilled and competent when interacting with a friend than a nonfriend. In the following sections, we will consider some features of early childhood friendships that make them such good contexts for learning.

 *Practice Tip*

Challenge Children

In one classroom, we watched while a sly teacher handed out three glue sticks to four children. She had more glue sticks in the box but didn't let the children see them. She waited a moment for the children to realize the situation and then asked them what they could do. Sure enough, the children came up with a way to share. This teacher created a problem so the children could learn by solving it. Problems can be opportunities.

 *Practice Tip*

Make Learning Easy

In a good early childhood classroom, we're always looking for ways to make learning easier for young children. We have child-sized scissors to make cutting easier. We have child-sized pitchers so children can learn how to pour, and after they've learned to pour, we give them larger pitchers for practice. How can we make learning to share and help others as easy as possible?

Child development research tells us to challenge children to use more prosocial behavior, starting with their closest friends. This is where the learning is easiest and performance the best. Once they can share and compromise with a friend, we can gently push them toward using these skills with other children. For example, if the class has difficulty sharing a favorite toy or activity, you can assign them in pairs of close friends so that they must take turns. You might give them an egg timer at first so they know when to switch turns. Once they can do this easily, you can mix up the pairs so that they learn to share with friends who are less close. Children will expand their prosocial behavior until it includes everyone in the class.

What if a child doesn't have a friend in the class to start with? Then that's the first thing you work on. Friends are needed to learn perspective-taking, empathy, and prosocial behavior.

Friends Provide Social Stability for Children

Friends can help each other deal with new situations.[56] In one study, toddlers were followed for several years in an early care and education program.[57] When they reached preschool age, a few moved to different child care programs. Some moved with a friend, some alone. The study found that, compared to those who moved alone, children who moved with a friend adjusted better and more quickly to the new setting. The familiarity of a friend appears to provide emotional support for children, much as it does for adults.

The loss of a friend can be very disruptive to a young child. Preschoolers have expressed loss and sadness several months after friends have moved away.[58] In one study a preschool-aged child whose friend moved away had difficulty getting along with peers.[59] This research shows us that early friendships are authentic. They have a substantial impact on children's emotions and their overall experience in the classroom.

 *Practice Tip*

Routines That Help Children Get to Know Each Other

When children arrive in the morning, a simple welcome song that lists all the children's names can help each one feel part of the group. You might sing "Let's Welcome Friends" (to the tune of "The Farmer in the Dell"):

> We're happy Ben is here,
> We're happy Ben is here,
> Let's clap and smile and welcome him,
> We're happy Ben is here.

Friends Help Children Learn to Get Along with Others

Social skills are behaviors that promote positive interactions among people. Some examples of important social skills for young children are sharing, taking turns, cooperating, and communicating clearly. For many reasons, some children have better social skills than others. Not surprisingly, children who have poor social skills often have a hard time getting along with other children. In a friendship, the one with greater social skills can help the one with fewer skills get along with others.[60] When the friend with greater social skills is part of a peer group, the one with fewer skills has an easier time becoming part of its activities. Even "rejected" children with some close friends have learned more social skills than "rejected" children without close friends. In other words, interactions between friends are opportunities for learning and improving social skills.

Friends Help Children Learn

In studies with older children, researchers wondered how friends would compare to nonfriends in different types of problem-solving tasks. Researchers found that, in comparison with nonfriends, the interactions of friends were marked by happier and more positive exchanges; more discussion, cooperation, and negotiation; and the pursuit of mutual rather than individual goals. As a result, friends explored each others' ideas much further than nonfriends and came up with more complex and elaborate solutions to problems.[61]

 *Practice Tip*

That's Why We Have a Dramatic Play Area!

You've seen children count on their fingers when they are still unable to count inside their heads. They do the same thing with perspective-taking. When they can't take the perspective of others "inside their head," they may use the dramatic play area to act out the role of others. Sometimes this is obvious. You might see an agitated preschooler reenact a family argument several times, taking the role of a different person each time. In this way, the preschooler gets an idea of how the argument felt to each person. A child doing this is working hard to understand the situation.

Child therapists often use dramatic play to help children process their understanding of family problems. The dramatic play corner is a learning center for social relations.[62]

 *Practice Tip*

The Case for Mixed-Age Groups

In family child care settings and some center-based programs, children have the opportunity over time to be the youngest child, middle child, and oldest child. Younger children can learn from older ones, and older children grow from the responsibility of modeling and teaching. It is not necessary for children to be the same age to teach each other valuable lessons in taking turns, perspective-taking, and prosocial behavior.

Although the study just described was done with school-age children, the same processes occur in the friendships of younger children and provide the same benefits. A good example is pretend play. Katherine and Moriah are deciding what kind of food they should cook in the "kitchen." Katherine wants to make cupcakes, while Moriah wants to make hamburgers. Katherine says that if they make cupcakes, they can have a pretend birthday party. Moriah says that if they make hamburgers, they can pretend they are at a fast-food restaurant. The two decide on a birthday party at the fast-food restaurant so they can make both cupcakes and hamburgers. This kind of negotiation takes place all the time in early childhood classrooms. Ideally, each child hears the other's thoughts and ideas, and together they come up with an activity that both can enjoy.

The discussion and negotiation that take place during play can lead to the role-playing of more complex and elaborate stories. Since friends want to maintain the relationship, they are motivated to learn social skills such as sharing, negotiation, cooperation, and conflict resolution. Because of the emotional security of a friendship, children also feel more comfortable about disagreeing and testing different ideas. This leads to the development of more complex thinking. Friendships benefit children by providing complex and challenging experiences that promote social, emotional, and cognitive growth.

Practice Tip

How We Help Children Build Social and Emotional Competence

Emotional competence is an important foundation for children's ability to explore, learn, and interact effectively with others. This includes an awareness of different emotional states—both in one's self and in others. Here are several examples:

We can label the child's feelings: "You're sad because Daddy had to leave."

We can describe our own feelings: "I'm frustrated because I can't open this jar."

We can interpret and give voice to the feelings of other children: "Mia screamed because she was scared when you ran up so fast."

We can model empathy and respect for others' feelings: "I know you want to stay outside and play; it's a beautiful morning. But we must go in for lunch now"; "You saw that Hector was hurt, so you got him his teddy bear, and that helped him feel better."

We can recognize and encourage prosocial behavior: "You put away all the blocks, so now we're ready to go outside to play"; "You saw that Nikki dropped her hat, and you gave it back to her. That was helpful"; "You gave Sean a turn on the bike. You are a good friend."

Friendships Help Foster Children's Prosocial Behaviors and Altruistic Values

Friendships may actually be necessary for children to learn how to truly understand and care about others' thoughts and feelings.[63] Parents and teachers impress upon children the importance of caring for others' feelings, but friendships give them the opportunity to develop this sense of caring through experience. In many ways, a consistent friendship is the essence of prosocial behavior (voluntary behavior intended to benefit another person). In fact, friendships take prosocial behavior a step further. Within a friendship children can develop altruistic values, that is, prosocial behavior motivated by concern for others rather than the expectation of personal reward. How do friendships do this?

When an adult interacts with a child, the adult usually represents an authority figure. Most of the time children understand that they must listen to the adult and comply. They seldom learn altruistic values doing things for adults because they think the acts are obligations. This is not meant to diminish the role of adults in the development of children's prosocial behavior. Adults help children learn how and when to act prosocially. Interactions with peers, on the other hand, teach children to use those prosocial skills because they want to, not because they are being watched by an adult. But why is this?

When interacting with adults or friends, children's motivations differ. In one study researchers observed preschool-aged children in their classrooms over a period of eighteen weeks.[64] They were interested in the children's explanations for complying with a request from an adult or child. For example, a teacher might ask a child to clean up, or a friend might ask for a turn with a toy. When these behaviors were observed, researchers asked the children why they had complied with the request. They discovered that when the request was from an adult, children were more likely to cite the teacher's power and authority as reasons for acting prosocially ("I must do what the teacher says"). In contrast, reasons for complying with a friend's request were more often based on perceptions of the other person's feelings or the importance of their friendship ("Because I like José"). This difference in motivation is particularly important in the context of disagreements between friends.[65]

Labeling Feelings

What We Saw

After some active movement and dancing, the teacher asked the children which dance they liked best. The discussion drifted to the difference between being active and being quiet. The teacher asked the children, "How are you feeling right now?" One child jumped up and down and exclaimed, "I'm feeling great!" Another child replied, "I'm getting tired." The teacher then asked, "How do you think Jill is feeling?" Several children replied, "Sad." The teacher asked, "How do you know she is feeling sad?" One child replied, "Tears coming down her face." Another said, "Crying." The teacher continued, "Why do you think she is sad?" Said one child, "She wanted someone to dance with her." "That's right," said the teacher. "She wanted to dance with Mary, but Mary wanted to dance alone." The children gathered around Jill and patted her on the back. Soon the group moved on to the next activity.

What It Means

How to observe others and interpret their internal experience is something children must learn. This smart teacher gives her children some guided practice, using ongoing activities as the emergent curriculum ("teachable moments"). Once children develop some skill at taking others' perspective, they are much more likely to act in a prosocial manner, just as this group does in comforting Jill.

Friends do not disagree any less often than nonfriends. In fact, young friends may disagree even more! However, friends deal with conflict differently. One research team observed preschool-aged friends and nonfriends during conflicts. The differences were clear: friends did not allow conflicts to become intense. They were more likely to compromise and more likely to continue playing together after the conflict.[66]

For children, negotiations that occur during play, particularly during conflicts, involve learning to understand the other person's perspective and feelings. This is certainly one of the most fundamental of all social skills. In play, children are often able to stretch beyond their own needs and compromise with playmates because they are highly motivated to maintain the friendship. Consider the difficulty and importance of these achievements by young children:

- The intellectual ability to understand another person's perspective and feelings.
- The altruistic desire to value another's feelings.
- The prosocial skills to manage a conflict that results in a mutual solution.

These achievements are attained largely within the social context of friendship. The desire to maintain the friendship provides the motivation to do the hard work of learning these skills. Prosocial thinking and behaving are far more likely when the child is involved with an equal rather than an adult authority figure.

The development of children's prosocial behaviors and friendships is a circular process: prosocial behavior leads to friendship, and friendship is the context for learning prosocial behavior. Prosocial children are desirable playmates because they can negotiate and compromise. When two children have played together successfully in the past, they continue to seek each other out. Each child's prosocial actions provide the building blocks for a relationship, and eventually their consistent contact develops into friendship. Prosocial behavior helps maintain the relationship as well, and having a friendship gives children a context for developing more advanced prosocial skills. As children experience problem solving, negotiation, and compromise within the friendship, they begin to care more about each other's thoughts and emotions, thus fostering altruistic values.

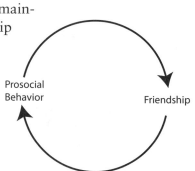

Prosocial Behavior

Friendship

 ## Practice Tip

Talk about Perspectives

Teachers can describe different perspectives for children. "Do the babies know what we have up here on the table? No, they can't see up here, can they?" Connecting language with children's actions and experiences is one of the keys to language development as well as to the development of skills such as perspective-taking.

One of the easiest places for a teacher to practice this skill is while reading to children. "Look at the picture. Juan doesn't see the raccoon behind him yet, right? Do you think Juan is afraid? No, not yet. But now look at this picture, where he turns and sees the raccoon. See Juan's face? How does Juan feel now?"

Great teachers also do this during ongoing social interactions in their classrooms: "Sara, this is Janie, and she is new here. She doesn't know anybody yet. How do you think she feels? What would make her feel better?" and "Sam, you grabbed the paint that Eric was waiting to use. How does Eric feel now?"

The Psychology of Prosocial Behavior

When we work with children, we try to keep in mind how each child has different skills and abilities that influence how he learns. For example, learning to use scissors can be difficult for young children, and how we help a patient, thoughtful child may differ from our approach with an impulsive, easily frustrated child. Similar thinking comes into play when teaching children how and why to behave prosocially with peers (and eventually within friendships). One of the main ways children differ—which strongly affects their peer relationships—is in their perspective-taking skills.

Perspective-Taking and Prosocial Behavior

From the second year of life, children's ability to understand the viewpoints of others improves. As noted, this skill turns out to be a crucial foundation for friendships. When children have this perspective-taking ability, they are much more likely to behave prosocially.[67]

One way to observe children's perspective-taking ability is to ask them about another person's point of view. For example, in one famous experiment, a child sits at one side of a table that has a model of three mountains of different sizes and colors at its center.[68] She can easily pick the photo that correctly shows her own view of the mountains. Then the child is asked to pick the photo that shows the view of a doll sitting at another side of the table. To answer correctly, she must be able to understand a viewpoint other than her own. When asked what the doll sees, most three-year-olds (and one-third of four-year-olds) point to their own view.[69] While children do better on this test if more familiar materials are used, such as Sesame Street characters, overall, many young children do not yet understand that others see things differently.

 *Practice Tip*

Reading to Children Is a Great Way to Enhance Perspective-taking

Choose stories that show children treating each other with respect and kindness. Read these stories individually and in small groups. When reading stories:

- Talk about the emotions shown by the characters.
- Ask the children how they think a character might be feeling.
- Ask the children what someone in the story could do to make a character feel better.

This ability doesn't just come naturally. All infants start out being egocentric—thinking others see things as they do. This does not mean they are bad or selfish, only that they need to learn. Gradually young children move away from egocentrism when their ability to see another's point of view improves. Separating one's viewpoint from another's is a necessary step toward acting prosocially.

Successful peer interactions require two kinds of perspective-taking skills, the social and the emotional. Social perspective-taking means sensing what another person is thinking or wants. For example, Mo has a big container of blocks and is making a spaceship with them. Maria sees Mo building and says, "That looks like fun." Mo replies, "Do you want to build too?" Here, Mo shows social perspective-taking by perceiving Maria's unstated wish to play with the blocks.

Emotional perspective-taking means sensing how another person feels. For example, Kiesha and Ashley are both trying to draw stars. Ashley is having trouble. She slams down her pencil and whines, "I can't do this!" Kiesha looks up from her drawing, walks around the table to Ashley, and says, "Here, let me show you." Kiesha appears to have understood that Ashley was frustrated.

One research study showed this very cleverly.[70] The study observed fifty-five sibling pairs, a preschooler (age three to five years) and a toddler (age one to two years). To test for skill in social perspective-taking, two adults played the game Secrets with the preschooler. Understanding who knew the secret and who didn't showed perspective-taking skill. To test for skill in emotional perspective-taking, the preschooler had to intuit a person's feelings from a picture story. After the tests, the sibling pair and their mother were moved to a playroom. The mother soon left the room, and the sibling pair was left alone with a stranger. At this point, the toddler usually became distressed.

The researchers wondered whether the preschooler's performance on the perspective-taking tasks would predict how much the preschooler would attempt to comfort the distressed toddler. The result? Older siblings who did well on the test of emotional perspective-taking gave more comfort to their toddler sibling.

 *Practice Tip*

What Do Teachers Do to Encourage Friendships, Especially for Children with Disabilities?

Children with some disabilities will tend to have fewer friendships than others in their early care and education programs. To help them, teachers must be actively involved. In one study of forty-five inclusive child care rooms, researchers observed the steps teachers took to help young children make friends.[71] The most common strategies were:

- Commenting on friends' play.
- Providing special materials or activities to encourage children to play together.
- Speaking or interpreting for a child so a friend could understand.
- Inviting two children to play together.

Some activities are better than others for encouraging friendship.[72] In one inclusive classroom, observers videotaped the social interaction of preschoolers in three activities: dramatic play, lunchtime, and using a computer. Surprisingly, they found the computer to be as good as the other two activities at encouraging talking and sharing between children. When matched with peers who were not disabled, children with disabilities had twice as much social interaction at the computer than they had at lunch or dramatic play! The key was *pairing* the children at the computer and the need for both children to work together—not just take turns—to play the computer learning game.[73]

Perspective-taking ability is critical to other prosocial behaviors such as sharing and cooperating. It helps children understand that "he wants to have a turn with the truck too" (sharing) or "she thinks it's better if I'm the daughter and she's the mom" (cooperating). For early childhood educators, awareness that some children are better at perspective-taking helps us to know how and when to teach children about prosocial behavior. If the children are just beginning to learn about the perspectives of others, we may need to use more coaching and mediation, give voice to the perspective of the other child, and explain how a compromise is good for both of them. If the children are more advanced, we can stand back, observe, and let them work things out on their own—intervening only if necessary.

Missing a Chance to Teach

What We Saw

Tasha walks over to the dramatic play area and says, "I want to wear the red shoes." Ann, the child with the shoes, says, "It's my turn. I have them on. Go away." Tasha grabs for the shoes and Ann screams, "Teacher!" Tasha sits on the floor and bursts into tears. The teacher says, "Give me a hug, Tasha. Now go find something else to do."

Why It Doesn't Work

The teacher does not validate Tasha's feelings or address her lack of skill at joining the play in a social manner.

Why We See This

Crying children cause upset; they disrupt the classroom. Teachers are busy and may look for the quickest, easiest way to stop it. But giving a hug and suggesting the child find another place to play does not help her make friends or learn to regulate her emotions and behavior.

What Would Work Better

This is a teachable moment. The teacher could have validated and labeled Tasha's emotions. "Tasha, you are *so* frustrated because you wanted those red shoes. Let's look for different shoes to wear. And we can ask Ann if you can be next to wear the red ones."

Emotions and Prosocial Behavior

Emotions play a key role in the development of children's prosocial behaviors and altruistic motivation. For example, when we see a child fall and scrape his knee, we usually experience some distress. Feeling the same emotions as another person is called empathy. Empathy is a form of perspective-taking that involves an emotional response. How a person deals with this emotional response affects whether the person acts in a prosocial manner. Usually, we set aside our own distress and begin to feel concern for the child. This concern leads us to comfort the child.

Some children respond in this way, too, acting prosocially out of empathy. However, other children can be overwhelmed by the other child's pain. These children look for ways to relieve their own distress and often ignore the child who is hurt. It is no surprise that children who can handle their own distress are more likely to behave prosocially.[74]

Being able to stay calm and in control of emotions helps children get along with each other. In one study, a researcher showed a preschooler an attractive box, saying it had something special inside. Just when the child was about to open the box, she told him he had to wait because she "forgot something in the car." The child was told not to touch the box until she returned—a difficult task for most preschoolers. After a few minutes she returned. Meanwhile, the child was being observed through a one-way window. Researchers found that children who were better able to manage their emotions, shown by not touching the box, were reported by their teachers as being more prosocial and better liked by their peers.[75]

The ability to manage emotions, known as self-regulation (see next chapter), helps children get along with each other. For example, Damon and Alicia both want to use the only tricycle on the playground. Although disappointed that he won't get to ride first, Damon decides to give Alicia the first turn. He knows that he'll get the next turn. Distress is common during conflicts between young children. Much like their ability to deal with empathic distress, children who can manage their emotions during conflicts are more likely to share or cooperate. Being aware of children's abilities to manage their own desires and emotions helps us know how and when to intervene.

 *Practice Tip*

> ## Scaffolding
>
> Scaffolding, a key teaching skill, means helping children in a way that lets them perform more competently. Anytime we suggest a solution to a child, we are scaffolding: "Perhaps you two can use this timer to take turns" or "Jason, you could help us by bringing the waste basket."
>
> We are also scaffolding when we *ask* about a solution: "Shanna and Maria, can you two think of a way to take turns with the wagon?" Even if they can't find a way, we don't take over. We do no more than necessary to promote competence. As they learn to settle their disagreements on their own, Shanna and Maria need fewer suggestions. Knowing how much scaffolding to provide requires that we observe children and know their abilities well. (All great teaching is individualized and begins with observation.)

How Teachers Can Support Friendship and Prosocial Behavior

First friendships and prosocial behaviors often develop hand-in-hand in the early childhood setting. Teachers can promote prosocial behavior in young children and their ability to establish and maintain friendships. Much of the research on this topic examines the link between parent–child relationships and peer relationships, but the findings likely apply to other caregivers, too, including early childhood teachers.

Creating a Sensitive and Responsive Relationship with the Child

Research has shown that children are more accepted by peers when their parents are warm, responsive, and in tune with their children.[76] In contrast, children tend to have more difficulty getting along with peers when parental interactions are hostile and overcontrolling. In other words, an adult–child relationship that involves listening to one another, cooperating, and displaying mutual enjoyment provides a model for interacting with others.[77]

In the early childhood setting, a warm relationship with children increases the effectiveness of all teaching strategies: the child thinks, "I am important to you. What you tell me or ask me to do is important, and I will listen."

Not Being Specific Enough

What We Saw

Teachers often tell frustrated or angry children to "use your words." This is a great idea, except sometimes the child doesn't know which words to use!

What Would Work Better

Sometimes we need to teach them the right words: "Tell Mia you don't like it when she pushes," or "Ask Leila if you can borrow one of her crayons."

Overemphasizing Rewards

What We Saw

Using rewards for prosocial behavior might be necessary as a first step for many children. But if stickers or even just praise is overused, children may act prosocially simply to gain the reward. Since overusing rewards can hinder the development of altruism, we should curtail their use as children's abilities improve.

What Would Work Better

Use cause-and-effect statements instead of rewards: "When you gave Kim a turn, it really made him happy." Or draw attention to the internal rewards of prosocial behavior, so children become self-rewarding: "I could tell you felt very grown up when you solved that problem yourself."

Modeling Socially Skilled Behavior

Modeling means acting the way we want the children to act, so they can learn by observing us. For example, when drawing we can ask, "Would you please pass me a blue crayon?" Over time, they will begin to copy your polite behavior. When playing a game, we can model cooperation by saying, "First you have a turn, and then I'll go next."

Reinforcing Socially Appropriate Behaviors

By reinforcing appropriate behaviors, children come to understand the types of behavior we value. For example, we can say to them, "Sharing the toy made both of you happy." Often children do not notice when they are sharing or taking turns or otherwise using social skills. By pointing out these behaviors and their effects on themselves and others, we help them become more aware of their prosocial skills. Then they can use them more consciously.

 *Practice Tip*

Using Puppets and Dolls to Teach Prosocial Skills

Dolls, puppets, stuffed animals, and play figures are wonderful tools for demonstrating social skills with young children. You can use these props to enact a scenario that represents a frequent, troublesome behavior in the classroom or an issue that one or more children are experiencing in their lives. Puppets and dolls help the children see the situation from a new perspective. And because everyone is calm, they allow for problem-solving discussions. For instance, if the children in your classroom are having trouble sharing toys, you might act out a similar situation during circle time using stuffed animals. Here's an example: Sparky was playing with the ball Kitty brought from home. Kitty saw him and ran after him, yelling, "It's mine—give it back." How do you think Kitty felt? What was Sparky feeling? Do you have any ideas for how they might work this out? (For more ideas on using this technique, see Trisha Whitney's *Kids Like Us: Using Persona Dolls in the Classroom* [Redleaf Press, 1999]).

Teaching Children How to Stay Calm

As discussed earlier, peer conflicts can involve intense emotional reactions, especially for young children just beginning to develop social skills with peers. Many of these children do not yet know how to manage their frustration and anger. This can lead to hitting or even a tantrum. In these situations, we can teach children strategies to stay calm (see the next chapter on self-regulation). But it is always helpful if we first give voice to the children's inner experience by saying out loud how they feel and why they might feel that way. Right away, this can make any situation more understandable and thus more manageable. We can then offer strategies to help them solve the problem or distract them from a situation that has no good solution. The following two strategies are particularly useful in fostering children's perspective-taking skills.

Coaching Children

Coaching is a direct form of teaching children about prosocial behavior. When we coach children, we help them see what they are doing and how their actions affect other people; we help them see options. Let's say you notice that when Miles sees a toy he wants, he simply tries to take it, even if another child is playing with it. So you take him aside and tell him, "Reiko was still using that bucket. She gets mad when you take her toys and doesn't want to play with you. Maybe you can ask if she will share. Can you try that?" Of course, coaching is not appropriate for all children, particularly younger children, and must be tailored to each child's abilities.

Talking about How Others Feel

What We Saw

Two children were helping to care for the classroom gerbils. The teacher instructed one child to dump out the water bottle and fill it with fresh water. "They're so happy to have fresh water," she said. Another child got out some sunflower seeds, and the teacher said, "They like sunflower seeds as a treat." The teacher then asked the children to sit on the floor, feet touching, and form a circular barrier. She put the gerbil in a clear, plastic exercise ball and set it in the circle. One child asked, "How come he's not moving?" The teacher explained, "He knows

*what to do. He's been in this ball before. He just woke up and
must be tired." Another child said, "He's scared!" The teacher
replied, "Yes, he might be a bit scared to be outside his safe
cage." The gerbil started to move in the ball, and the children
giggled and smiled at each other.*

What It Means

The teacher used the gerbils to help the children understand
how another living creature might feel about hunger, thirst,
new situations, or just waking up. The children were learning
perspective-taking and empathy. In this situation, the key
was not just playing with a classroom pet, but observing the
pet, imagining how it must feel, and providing words for its
feelings.

Talking about Emotions

Researchers have found that talking about emotions and feelings while
conversing with children fosters their perspective-taking skills.[78] This is
because adults label emotions for children ("Sam is sad because he lost
his ball"); explain how their behavior can affect another person ("When
you pull on Angela's hair, it really hurts her, just like when your hair is
pulled"); and encourage them to talk about emotions and their causes.

Although most of this research was based on children and their
mothers, very likely it can tell us about good early childhood practice
in general. In one study,[79] researchers taped the conversations between
mothers and their three-year-olds at home. The researchers were particularly interested in conversations about feelings and their many sources.
They wanted to see how conversations in the home influenced children's
later perspective-taking skills. Later, when the children were six years
of age, they were asked to listen to a picture story in which the main
character would start out feeling one way but feel differently by the end
of the story. Each child was asked to say how the person in the story felt
at the beginning and at the end. Researchers found that when conversations in the home at age three included more discussions about feelings
and the causes of those feelings, the children did better on the emotional-
understanding task at age six. This suggests that conversations about
feelings and their causes can help children to develop their social and
emotional perspective-taking skills. Thus, talking about how the pet

bunny feels and how a character in a picture book feels is a crucial form of instruction for this age group.

Righting a Wrong without Talking with the Children about the Behavior

What We Saw

Four-year-old Alex took a toy car away from Micah. The teacher intervened by taking the toy from Alex and giving it back to Micah.

Why It Doesn't Work

The teacher's action repeats the child's problematic behavior—taking the toy away. It leaves both children angry and doesn't teach prosocial behavior.

Why We See This Practice

Seeing a child take away a toy makes adults uncomfortable because it violates fairness. We want to right the wrong. But if we do, we might miss this opportunity to promote emotional perspective-taking and prosocial skills.

What Would Work Better

Describe the situation and the emotional context. "Alex, you wanted the car so you took it away from Micah. That made Micah mad because he wanted to play with it too." This explanation helps both children understand what happened and recognize the emotional perspective of the other. Then suggest a more acceptable behavior: "Maybe you can ask Alex to push the car to you, and you can push it back to him." This allows the children to play with the toy together. It promotes positive social interaction and satisfies the desires of both children.

The researchers in that study were interested not only in the mothers' talk about feelings, but also in the children's part. We should keep this in mind in our conversations with children. In addition to our own contributions to conversations about feelings, we should encourage children to do their own thinking and talking about them. Learning to label emotions is basic to understanding them in ourselves or in others. Using words to label emotions—both the child's own emotions and the emotions of others—is a kind of direct, verbal instruction that every child needs. Once children have a word for something, they can begin to bring it under conscious control. If children don't receive this instruction at home, receiving it in their early care and education program is even more important.

Equally important to labeling emotions is learning to apply labels to describe how actions can cause feelings and vice versa. Research studies have found that some children seldom hear sentences at home such as "When you do [action], your sister feels [emotion]."[80] These children lag in perspective-taking ability when they enter an early childhood program, but benefit more than others from hearing this type of explanation from their teachers. Learning these skills promotes successful peer interactions that can lead to friendships.

PROMISING PRACTICE

Letting Children Solve Problems Without Your Help

What We Saw

During free-choice time, five trays with playdough and utensils were available. At first no one was interested, but then six children rushed to the table at once. One child did not have a tray to use for playdough. Cornelius looked up from his tray and said to Eric, the child without a tray, "Hey, you can play with me." The two children stood together by the tray and shared the playdough. The teacher, who had been watching nearby, smiled and said, "That was very nice of you, Cornelius." The children continued to play together in a cooperative manner.

What It Means

Sometimes teachers have to refrain from jumping in too soon to solve problems. If the teacher had done so here, the children would have missed an opportunity to practice and perfect their prosocial abilities. The decision about whether to step in and solve the problem, give the children a hint (or some other assistance), or watch and do nothing is based on knowledge of the children's abilities. Smart teachers know how to match the challenge to the child and resist the temptation to be in charge at all times, trying to solve all problems. This teacher was clearly paying very close attention and was quick to highlight (and thus reinforce) the children's competent prosocial behavior.

Children Must Be Given the Chance to Resolve Their Conflicts

As teachers, we often keep a watchful eye on children's interactions with peers. But researchers have found that the way we monitor children can either help or hinder their learning peer interaction skills.

In one study, for example, researchers asked parents to describe how they monitored their preschool-aged children's interactions with peers in the home.[81] Parents were classified as using direct monitoring (closely watching the children and often participating in the activities) or indirect monitoring (checking on the children but remaining mostly uninvolved). The researchers then went to the children's child care programs, found out how well liked they were by other children, and found out which children the teachers felt were more hostile and aggressive. Results showed that peers preferred children who were indirectly monitored, and teachers perceived them as less aggressive and hostile. The researchers reasoned that the indirectly monitored children had more opportunities to practice different prosocial skills and problem-solving strategies because their mothers were less likely to immediately solve disagreements for them. In turn, the children were able to transfer these skills from home to the child care setting. This study tells us that although we need to monitor children for safety at all times, we also need to give them the chance to resolve their conflicts themselves if able. As noted before, children's skill and level of understanding should influence how, and how much, we intervene in their interactions.

To learn how to get along with peers, children need the support of adults, but they also need opportunities to practice skills on their own. Adults set the stage by modeling, reinforcing, and coaching appropriate social behavior. Children then develop their social skills during interactions with friends. Meanwhile, adults continue to monitor their progress. Having cooperative peer relationships and warm friendships gives children an optimal environment for learning. Children can learn from each other and provide each other with companionship and emotional support.

Further Reading

On Research

Dunn, J. 2004. *Children's friendships: The beginnings of intimacy.* Oxford: Blackwell.

Kemple, K. 1991. Research in review: Preschool children's peer acceptance and social interaction. *Young Children* 46 (5): 47–54.

On Practice

Bullok, J. 1993. Lonely children. *Young Children* 48 (6): 53–57.

Greenberg, P. 1992. Promoting positive peer relations. *Young Children* 47 (4): 51–59.

Honig, A., and D. Wittmer. 1996. Helping children become more prosocial: Ideas for classrooms, families, schools, and communities. Part II. *Young Children* 51 (2): 62–70.

Katz, L. G., and D. E. McClellan. 1997. *Fostering children's social competence: The teacher's role.* Washington, D.C.: National Association for the Education of Young Children.

McGlurg, L. G. 1998. Building an ethical community in the classroom: Community meeting. *Young Children* 53 (2): 30–35.

Whitney, T. *Kids like us: Using persona doll stories in the classroom.* St. Paul: Redleaf Press.

Wittmer, D., and A. Honig. 1994. Encouraging positive social development in young children. *Young Children* 49 (5): 4–12.

Children's Books

Bottner, B. 1980. *Mean Maxine.* New York: Pantheon.

Carlson, N. 1994. *How to lose all your friends.* New York: Viking.

Hutchins, P. 1993. *My best friend.* New York: Greenwillow Books.

Lionni, L. 1963. *Swimmy.* New York: Pantheon.

Lionni, L. 1985. *It's mine!* New York: Alfred A. Knopf.

Munsch, R. 1999. *We share everything!* New York: Scholastic.

Rohmann, E. 2002. *My friend rabbit.* Brookfield, Conn.: Roaring Brook Press.

Zolotow, C., and A. Lobel. 1963. *The quarreling book.* New York: Harper and Row.

When Teachers Reflect: *The Conditions for Altruism to Grow*

Some adults—and some children—want to be rewarded for everything they do. This shows a lack of *altruism* (doing something simply because it is right or because it helps another person). However, there are plenty of opportunities for altruistic and prosocial activities in your program's daily schedule.

You might begin by recognizing all the children's positive behaviors. When they offer to help you, thank them, and tell them that you like having help. Remark on such generosity when you see it among the children. Circle time is a good time for the children themselves to recognize the kindnesses of their peers. Be prepared to notice something positive about every child, so no one feels excluded.

You might even adopt a cause for the children to champion. They could collect pennies to buy toys for a homeless shelter or make birthday cards for people at a retirement home. Doing something voluntarily without reward is good practice in altruism.

When Teachers Reflect: *Distressed Lives*

Some children experience severe distress in their homes or neighborhoods. For them, focusing attention outside themselves—empathizing—is difficult. How should we adjust our teaching for these children? Since learning empathy may come more slowly for them, we could adjust our expectations of them. We could also make our classrooms peaceful havens, where they might feel secure enough to experience the care of others and thus learn to tend others' cares. As seen in chapter 1, we risk exploring only when we feel secure.

This point applies to child care teachers too. When problems arise, we have less energy to attend to the needs of others. As we mature, we are better able to set aside our problems for the time being and pay full attention to the children in our care. Giving full attention to another person may be the kindest gift you can give. By working to improve our own lives, we lay the foundation for better teaching.

Letter to Parents

Did You Know?
Children who learn to play well and work well with others in early childhood tend to do better in these and other areas of their lives as they grow older.

Did You Know?
Children must *learn* to understand the perspective of others. Perspective-taking is a skill that helps children get along.

Did You Know?
The teachers in our program help the children learn to solve their everyday disagreements, negotiate their problems, and handle their emotions—all of which are necessary skills for making friends and working well in a group.

It's So Much More Than Snacktime
When sitting at the table with the children during snacktime, our teachers model the positive behaviors we want the children to learn. They encourage the children to use good manners, take turns, and listen to each other. At every opportunity, our early childhood program teaches:

- Helpful behaviors (skills of living together cooperatively).
- Emotion recognition (putting feelings into words).
- Empathy (understanding the feelings of others).

We care for the whole child, building a foundation for happy, socially comfortable individuals.

You are welcome to observe our program at any time and to ask about our teaching methods.

From *Social and Emotional Development: Connecting Science and Practice in Early Childhood Settings* (Redleaf Press, 2007).

3

Why We Play Simon Says
Learning Self-Regulation

Usually the four-year-olds can go right outside to play, but today they must wait for the teachers. Becoming impatient, they break out of line and run around the room. Noah wants to be the first to get a swing, so he throws on his jacket and hurries to the head of the line at the door. Then, while waiting, he turns his back to the door so he can't see the playground and sings a song to himself.

What Is Self-Regulation, and Why Is It Important?

Despite his obvious excitement, Noah controls himself with little or no guidance from his teachers. Some children have learned ways to distract themselves while waiting. Other children become so emotional that they misbehave or even throw a temper tantrum.

Noah's mature behavior reflects his developing capacity for self-regulation. *Self-regulation* is the process of exercising control over one's actions (for example, becoming less impulsive), thinking processes (for example, focusing attention and planning activities), and emotions (for example, managing frustration). Growing up is largely the story of gaining control of our own lives. Children are born needing nearly constant help regulating themselves, including temperature and emotions. But even as infants they begin to control their own physiological states (for example, learning to calm themselves when they're too aroused) and gradually learn to control their thinking, focus, emotions, and behaviors.[82]

The good news is that we know a great deal about helping children learn self-regulation. If you help children improve their self-control as preschoolers, it not only leads to a more pleasant classroom for you, but it also could have a profound impact on their lives.

Teaching a Strategy for Impulse Control

What We Saw

The teacher is at the puzzle table with a group of children. Nita grabs at Kyle's partly finished puzzle. The teacher intervenes, "Nita, you have to wait until Kyle is done." Nita gets up from her chair and knocks it over. "I see that you are angry," says the teacher, "but you have to wait your turn. Come and sit with me, Nita. We can do another puzzle while you wait." Nita sits down, still fussing, but the teacher is able to engage her in another puzzle.

What It Means

Nita is strongly motivated to work the puzzle, but she lacks enough *self-control* to wait her turn. The ability to inhibit one's own actions does not come naturally to children; they must learn it. Children need our help in developing strategies of self-control. The strategy used here focuses attention on an alternate activity (a different puzzle). The child needs the teacher's help to use this strategy today, but with practice Nita will learn to use it independently to regulate herself. She will have learned to *delay gratification* on her way to an eventual goal. This is no small achievement.

The Benefits of Self-Regulation

Self-regulation is an important ability for children in many situations. Researchers have found that preschool-aged children who are better at regulating their own behavior are more prosocial and better liked by peers.[83] It's easy to imagine why children who cannot control their impulses might be less liked. Their lack of emotional or impulse control can lead to diminished cooperation and behavior problems such as non-compliance with adults or fights with peers. About 10 to 15 percent of preschool-aged children exhibit mild to moderate behavior problems, usually involving poor self-regulation.[84] Children with a limited ability to inhibit their impulses are more likely to be diagnosed with conduct disorder or attention-deficit/hyperactivity disorder.[85]

One study tested the link between preschoolers' ability to self-regulate and their social behavior.[86] Researchers began by measuring their ability to self-regulate at the start of the year. They asked teachers to rate the children's conduct problems, such as fights with peers and non-compliance with adults, both at the beginning of the year and one year later. The results showed that the poor self-regulators had more conduct problems, both at the beginning of the year and one year later, just before entering elementary school. We might wonder what the early childhood teachers could have done to help them learn self-regulation that year.

Self-regulation also predicts success throughout a child's lifespan. According to research, children who were better at self-regulation in the preschool years have more self-confidence and self-esteem; better cognitive and social skills; and more independence, better academic performance, and greater ability to handle stress and frustration during adolescence.[87] By observing which four-year-olds have greater control of their impulsive behavior, researchers can predict those most likely to use alcohol and other drugs as adolescents.[88] Even more amazing is the fact that better self-regulation during early childhood predicts occupational success and general life satisfaction during adulthood.[89]

PROMISING PRACTICE

Music Helps Control the Pace of an Activity

What We Saw

The children are in the large activity room, and Juan is getting a little wild. He goes over to the rocking boat and starts pushing it back and forth. Teacher Sally asks him, "Juan, would you like to rock in the boat?" He climbs right in. She makes a general pronouncement, "Are there any other riders in the boat?" Three other children get in. Teacher Sally begins rocking them back and forth at a steady pace, singing, "Row, row, row your boat. . . ." The children smile, and some sing along.

What It Means

If *unfocused energy* can be a problem, *structured energy* is a good thing. This teacher helps Juan learn to organize and structure his play, which can help prevent behavior problems. More importantly, it helps Juan learn self-control. The teacher uses song to set a pace for rocking the boat. Songs are good tools for helping children learn to control the pace of their actions. Teachers can use songs every day to help children develop more control.

LEARNING SELF-REGULATION IN THE DRAMATIC PLAY AREA

Dramatic play has long been seen as an effective way for children to learn and practice social skills.[90] Recent research shows that dramatic play is also effective at teaching self-regulation to impulsive children. This makes sense. Successful dramatic play requires cooperation, joint planning, and goal-setting among children—all functions that require a great deal of self-regulation.

One study followed a group of three- to four-year-olds in their early childhood classrooms to see which children showed the greatest improvement in self-control. From fall to spring, self-control was measured by observing the children during cleanup time and circle time.[91] A strong predictor of improved self-regulation—particularly for the children who were most impulsive in the fall—was their degree of engagement in complex, socio-dramatic play. In this kind of play, two or more children must interact—not just play alongside each other—and the play must include make-believe and verbal interaction that goes on for some time. Researchers evaluated the play by observing two areas in each classroom, the playhouse and the large block area. In the study's classrooms the playhouse and large block area were joined, allowing children to easily combine props from both areas. (According to Heidemann and Hewitt[92] this room arrangement has been found to encourage complex, make-believe play.)

Early childhood teachers can encourage complex, dramatic play by providing new props such as those for a restaurant, grocery store, or bus trip. Elaborating on children's ideas helps sustain the make-believe. For example, "If Juan is the bus driver, do you have to give him a coin when you get on?"

How Self-Regulation Develops

For people who work with young children every day, using the words "self-regulation" and "early childhood" in the same sentence may seem like a contradiction! Young children tend to be impulsive, and many are quite dependent on adults to structure their actions. But the foundation of self-regulation is built in early childhood, and early childhood programs are well suited to helping children develop this invaluable skill. We will describe how children develop three types of self-regulation:

1. Behavioral: the ability to inhibit actions.
2. Cognitive: the ability to plan.
3. Emotional: the ability to regulate emotions.

Behavioral Self-Regulation (Impulse Control)

The regulation of personal actions, or *impulse control*, includes both the ability *not* to do something and the ability to control the speed at which something is done. Young children first learn how to perform an action but only later learn how to regulate it. Until they can learn to inhibit their actions—to slow down or stop an action and give themselves the chance to think—they will be unable to choose between alternative actions. No inhibition means no choice and no planning.

According to Maccoby,[93] most infants seven months or younger will reach out for an unusual object. But starting around eight months, most begin to show wariness about strange objects. This is the beginning of the ability to control an impulse or action. At age three, most children cannot successfully play Red Light, Green Light. They can't stop themselves from going whenever any light comes on! But by age five, most children can give a different response for the red light.

Children also learn to regulate the speed of their actions. Motor skills are initially learned at the speed that is easiest for the body. With time and practice, the child develops the ability to perform the same skill at both slower and faster speeds. For example, three-year-olds cannot consistently draw lines slowly. They seem to have only one speed. But they get better at this skill each year up through at least age six.

◆ GAMES THAT DEVELOP IMPULSE CONTROL

Traditional games:

- Red Light, Green Light
- Simon Says
- Mother May I
- London Bridge
- Ring Around the Rosie
- Freeze Tag
- Ready, Set, Go! (child must wait for "Go!")

Freeze songs:

- "Pause" from *Movin'* by Hap Palmer
- "My Pony, Stop and Go" from *Look at My World* by Kathy Poelker

Song that teaches behavioral inhibition:

- "B-I-N-G-O"

Songs that teach a regular beat or rhythm:

- "Miss Mary Mack"
- Clapping to the beat of any music

Activities that involve changes in pace:

- Moving to music in different tempos (fast/slow)
- "Can you scurry like a monkey? Now lumber like an elephant"
- Pretending to swim through an ocean of molasses
- "The Wind-Up Toy Factory" from *Look at My World* by Kathy Poelker
- "Let's tiptoe quietly past the sleeping dinosaur"

As with other aspects of child development, the fact that we can describe the normal ages for the development of self-regulation is probably due, at least in part, to natural maturation. In fact, the development of self-regulation in early childhood coincides with growth spurts in the frontal lobes of the child's brain.[94] The human brain continues to grow basic structures and functional abilities for the first several years of life.

Children's increasing self-regulation probably reflects the new abilities of the growing brain.

However, there is another, more interesting theory. Scientists now believe that early experiences can actually change the basic structures of the brain as it forms. Some children have more opportunities to experience and develop self-regulation while their brains are rapidly changing. If so, this helps explain the research finding that early experiences of learning self-regulation can predict occupational success and general well-being decades later.[95] This chapter summarizes the kinds of experiences that can make this difference.

Impulse Control and Compliance

It makes sense that when children are more capable of controlling their actions, they are more capable of complying with adult demands. When we ask them to wait their turn, wait in line, or let others use the crayons, for example, we are asking for impulse control.

By age two, many children are clearly compliant and evidence the self-control that makes it possible. This is surprising in at least one respect: in the toddler years children are developing their sense of autonomy (the desire to be in charge of themselves) and independence. This drive is precisely why they use the word "no" so much. Nothing asserts their selfhood as clearly as *No!*

Yet, in the toddler years, adults are increasing their demand that young children get along with others and follow the rules of group living, rather than getting their own way. Thus, adults' *socialization pressure* comes into direct conflict with toddlers' drive for autonomy. Many people refer to this conflict as the Terrible Twos.

Much of the adult–child conflict in this period can be limited by letting children make their own decisions whenever possible and by exercising socialization pressure selectively. At the same time, the conflict presents a great opportunity to foster children's self-regulation. The best behaved children have internal control; adult control is unnecessary.

 **Practice Tip**

Replace *Don't* with *Do*

To foster impulse control, phrase sentences to create positive images in the child's mind. Instead of saying "Don't run," try rephrasing your request: "Use walking feet." Instead of "Don't hit," try saying "Soft touches." You can take it one step further by modeling the action while saying the words. Instead of "Don't pull the cat's tail," try "Pet the kitty like this." When you tell and show a child the right way to do something, you are a teaching a new skill. Not so with "don't" phrases. Monitor how often you say "don't," and force yourself to rephrase your directives in positive terms.

PROMISING PRACTICE

Routines Help Children Learn Self-Control

What We Saw

The teacher sits at a table set for lunch. Several children are chattering as the last child finishes washing his hands and sits down. She raises her hand in the air. The children quiet down and then raise their hands. The teacher says, "Ready? 1, 2, 3 . . ." and they all sing a thank-you song. She then picks up a plate of potatoes and passes it to the child on her right. "We'll pass the bread and potatoes first, then the fruit." Each child takes a share and passes the plate to the next child. When each plate has been passed around the table, the children begin to eat.

What It Means

The mealtime routine at this center is consistent in each room. It is a part of the process of *socialization*—teaching children how to act in social situations. Children are learning their table manners, but they also are learning to delay gratification, control their impulses, and plan their actions. Because the mealtime routine is the same for every meal, the children know what to expect

("I will eat soon") and how to act (wait, sing, serve, eat). The predictability helps them comply with the social requirements. It's not just manners they are learning, but also self-regulation.

If we take into account that young children have serious difficulty with impulse control, then we may need to reinterpret their misbehavior. Is it defiance or simply a lack of control (either one might be accurate)? We know that three-year-olds struggle with Red Light, Green Light because they can't seem to stay put whenever *any* light comes on. What happens when you tell a three-year-old, "Don't pull the cat's tail"? You have actually planted an idea, and *any* idea (like *any* light) is hard to resist. We shouldn't be so surprised when he reaches down—impulsively—and pulls the cat's tail.

Of course, whether a child complies with an adult's request depends on more than just the ability to inhibit impulses. As we saw in chapter 1, for example, children are more compliant with adults to whom they are close.[96] Children are also more compliant when the rules are clear and consistent. In turn, clear and consistent rules help children become more autonomous and self-regulating.[97]

MISTAKEN PRACTICE

Children Are Told Repeatedly to Stand Still in Line While Waiting to Go Outside.

Why It Doesn't Work

The caregiver isn't teaching the children how to accomplish this.

Why We See This Mistaken Practice

Saying "Don't do that" or "Stand still!" is obvious. Turning the situation into a teaching opportunity—what to teach children to do while waiting—requires some thought.

What Would Work Better

Show the children how to distract themselves while waiting. "Waiting is hard. Why don't we sing a song while we wait?"

CAN WE TEACH CHILDREN TO BE LESS IMPULSIVE?

A very interesting experiment was carried out with a group of adolescent offenders in jail.[98] Based on a delay-of-gratification test, all were highly impulsive. Half the group was exposed to an older, more mature inmate—soon to be released—who modeled less impulsive behavior. During the experiment the role model made delayed choices and drew attention to them with comments such as "I can wait for that." As a result, impulsive inmates who interacted with the role model became much less impulsive than the other half of the group. This evidence suggests that adolescents can learn to be less impulsive by observing a role model. The same may hold true for preschoolers whose impulsiveness is not yet a long-standing trait.

As teachers, you are the most influential role models for children. In using this method it is important not only to make thoughtful, measured decisions yourself, but also to explain them clearly to the children. "I'm really excited, but I know I have to wait," or "I'm hungry, but I can wait until everyone is served." In this way, children not only see their teacher practice self-regulation, but also learn what she is thinking that helps control her impulses.

Cognitive Self-Regulation

Young children are impulsive not only in their behaviors, but also in their thinking and decision making. Some have difficulty focusing on anything for long. Most fail to plan their activities. Nevertheless, once children begin to account for more than just the present, once they develop a sense of the future, they can start using *reflective problem solving*. In other words, they can think ahead about the pros and cons of actions; they can plan rather than merely decide on impulse. They can also begin to *delay immediate gratification,* turning down a short-term gain in service of a longer-term goal.

These skills are important for children's futures. Those with a low ability to plan and organize their actions and a low ability to stay on task—elements of cognitive self-regulation—tend to have more social and behavioral problems in elementary school.[99]

Reflective Problem Solving

As they grow, children become more reflective and less impulsive not only in their behavior, but also in their decision making. This is helpful because children who take longer to think through a task or problem tend to make fewer errors.[100] A reflective approach to problem solving usually emerges by about age five.

Before they can even begin problem solving, however, children must be able to focus on an activity instead of jumping from one thing to the next. *Attentional control* grows throughout the preschool years in most children. According to research, children from ages two to three roughly double the longest span of uninterrupted playtime with a single object, from thirty seconds at age two to almost a minute at age three.[101] Children who can remain on task tend to be better at reflective problem solving. Children who learn to focus their attention earlier do better when older. One study showed that focused attention at nine months of age predicted the ability to control oneself in the preschool years.[102]

HOW WE HELP CHILDREN LEARN TO PLAN

There are many strategies you can use to help children learn to plan.

Scaffolding

As we learned in chapter 2, scaffolding helps a child accomplish a task with just enough support. You withdraw your support gradually so the child learns to do it independently. For example, if you help a child develop a plan for her play *without taking over*, she can improve her ability to organize. To help a child learn to plan, you can:

- Model a plan of action: "I'd like to build a castle with the blocks. First I need to make the walls."
- Draw the child into your ideas: "Will you make the wall on the other side? It needs to be this tall."
- Draw out the child's ideas: "What else can we put on the castle?"

Developmental Matching

Just as children can focus their attention and control their impulses for only a short time at first, they can make only simple plans at first. Later they can anticipate and construct more complex plans. Thus, we shouldn't expect more than is warranted at their current level of ability. To do so would only ensure failure. But respecting children's current ability doesn't mean low expectations. With time, we should demand a bit more.

Great teaching starts by observing children with sufficient care to know their current abilities. Our demands will then match their developmental level. Slowly we demand a bit more. For example, at first we might ask them to place a drinking cup in front of each chair. Later in the year, we might ask them how many cups are needed at the class table for lunch.

Foreshadowing

Warning children that cleanup time approaches is one example of *foreshadowing*—helping children think about what will happen next. Foreshadowing, or future planning, gives them time to end the current activity and prepare for the next one. Here are two examples:

- Asking a child, "What would happen if you put a big block on top of a small block on a tower?" This helps the child think about the effects of her actions.
- Telling a toddler, "I'm going to pick you up now so we can change your diaper." This promotes the child's ability to predict what will happen next and also builds trust and security.

Routines

Having a consistent daily routine—breakfast, free play, clean up, circle, story, outdoor play, etc.—helps children learn to predict what will happen next. Predictability helps them learn to plan. It also helps them wait, when they must, because they know that one activity always follows another.

Modeling

You can provide a powerful model for the children by demonstrating self-regulation of your own behavior while explaining aloud what you are doing. For example, you might demonstrate:

- Reflective problem solving: when trying to reach supplies on a high shelf, you might say, "I can't reach the shelf. I could stand on a chair, but these chairs are wobbly. I had better use the stepladder."

♦ Delayed gratification: when the meal cart arrives, you might say, "I'm really hungry, but I can wait until we wash our hands and all sit down."

♦ Future planning: as you prepare materials for an art project, you might say, "There is room for three children to paint at this table, so I need to get three smocks, three brushes, and three paint cups."

Materials

Certain classroom materials can reinforce planning. Jigsaw puzzles, for example, are great for teaching children to plan an approach to a problem. First, you spread out the pieces face up. Then you find the straight-edged pieces and assemble them to create the frame. Next, you group the pieces by color and assemble the sections, either working inward from the frame or assembling distinctive units first.

A jigsaw puzzle is a good planning tool because it provides so much structure. But children need greater challenges to improve their abilities. Working with paint, playdough, or blocks is the opposite of doing puzzles, because there are many solutions, not just one. Moreover, the child is the one who must decide when a solution has been reached. Open-ended materials require the child to be much more organized. He must provide the structure.

A Planful Approach

The High/Scope® Curriculum approach, Plan–Do–Review, is a great example of how to help children think and make choices before they act.[103] During Planning Time, children are asked to choose which activity they will work on during Work Time. If the child leaves the area during Work Time and goes to another activity, the teacher may ask, "Are you changing your plan?" This approach makes the child aware that thinking should come before acting. Talking later with the children about what they accomplished reinforces the planful approach.

But, as always, children differ greatly. Some have learned to concentrate on a problem for some time before making a decision, while others are very impulsive. The impulsive children are not quicker at thinking and deciding. Rather, they neither observe nor think as carefully and, as a result, often fail to impose a plan of action on a problem.

We know, too, that children who think impulsively do not simply have shorter attention spans. We know this because they can often do structured activities, such as watching TV, for long periods. However, they generally have trouble with unstructured activities such as working with playdough, blocks, and finger paints. What's the difference? When watching TV, a rapid sequence of attention-grabbing events occurs automatically; no input from the child is needed. Unstructured activities, by contrast, require children to impose their own structure; they must develop a creative goal or plan of action. This is difficult for children who think impulsively; they cannot stay focused on these activities for long. Lack of focus is one of the key characteristics of children with attention-deficit/hyperactivity disorder (see When Teachers Reflect at the end of this chapter). As teachers, our role is to help children become more planful and creative with their toys and activities, to help them become more self-organizing.

The process of learning reflective problem solving, more than any other aspect of self-regulation, requires the guidance of caregivers and teachers. Some activities, such as baking, lend themselves to teaching this skill. Because baking involves several steps—reading the recipe, getting out the bowls and ingredients, measuring, pouring, stirring—children learn the importance of being planful when approaching a task. They learn that a plan is made up of a series of steps done one at a time, in order. (Use pictures on a board to show the steps.) In other words, smaller goals must be completed to accomplish a larger goal. This is a lesson in planfulness and self-organization.

There are opportunities throughout the day to teach children to plan their actions. For example, imagine two children trying to build a house with blocks. They start stacking blocks but can't seem to build what they want. This is the perfect moment to teach them about planning their activity: they are frustrated but not *too* frustrated. If you make sure not to impose your own ideas or to distract them if they are still thinking, you can offer suggestions about planning the construction: "Can you show me where the walls will be?" The other children should be a big part of this planning too: "Will you have a door? Where will it be?" When similar situations arise, you can then remind them of their previous planning strategies. As they get older, children become more adept at planning in different types of situations, and you can say less.

As with learning to inhibit actions, children need structure when first learning reflective problem solving. You can provide less support gradually as they increase their ability to structure their own decisions and actions. In this way, the children can become self-regulating.

HELPING CHILDREN BECOME MORE REFLECTIVE

As the children arrive in the morning, try asking them what they would like to do that morning. Be ready with suggestions, but give each child a solid chance to make a plan.

To get them thinking, ask them what supplies they will need to complete an activity. For example, when a child says, "I want to draw a picture," be prepared to ask questions that help the child plan. "What size paper do you want? Can you get the paper yourself? Are you planning on using crayons or markers?"

Talking to children about what will happen tomorrow also promotes reflection. Make them curious, make it interesting, and ask for their input. "Tomorrow we will paint our clay sculptures. Yao, what color will you paint yours tomorrow? What should we do so paint doesn't get on our clothes?"

Planning a field trip is another chance to strengthen reflective thinking. Asking the children to think about everything from name tags, to transportation, to snacks can result in an interesting session.

You can also use this type of conversation to let the children know what is expected of them: "When we are in the library, what can we do to help us stay very quiet until story time?" This helps them control their behavior.

Last, be sure to talk about the activity after it is over. Ask the children to recall the plan and then reflect on how well it worked out. "Did we get the sculptures painted okay? Did we spill much paint on ourselves? Were we able to keep quiet at the library?" Reviewing the plan after the event is an important part of reflective thinking.

PROMISING PRACTICE

Teaching Children to Reflect and Plan

What We Saw

The children have just finished circle time on the rug. As they transition to free-play time, the teacher asks Liz what she will do next. Liz says she would like to go to the block area. The teacher asks, "Do you have an idea of something you would like to build?" Liz answers, "Yes, I want to build a doghouse." The teacher asks if she needs to take anything else to the block area to help make the doghouse. Liz giggles and says, "I guess I should get some dogs from the farm set." Another child says, "Liz, will the dogs live alone after you build the house?" Liz answers, "No. Maybe I need some people to live with them. I'll get some little people too."

What It Means

The teacher used Liz's choice of the block area as a chance for the child to plan her playtime. The teacher's open-ended questions gave Liz a chance to think about what she would need. Liz is learning to plan her actions.

Delaying Gratification

As part of a psychological test, a preschooler is told he can have a small chocolate bar today or a larger chocolate bar tomorrow.[104] The chocolate bars are on the table; the choice is very real. Some children take the small bar, while others say they want to wait for the larger bar. This is a test of children's ability to *delay gratification*, another kind of cognitive self-regulation. It is amazing that such a simple test can predict so much about the child's behavior, both today and in the future.

The ability to delay gratification emerges around age three and a half. As children grow older, most get better at delaying rewards or desired actions, but there are wide differences among children the same age. Studies have shown that these differences are important for children's futures. Those who are better able to delay gratification come to feel a sense of mastery over their lives; what happens to them is not the result of mere luck.[105] This sense of mastery is also related to higher self-esteem and better mental health later in life.

How can adults help children learn to delay gratification? To begin with, we can provide them with a predictable environment. Learning to put off an immediate reward for a larger reward later is only possible when children trust the promise of a greater reward, that is, when they've had prior experience of success in delaying gratification. If children live in homes and classrooms where they cannot predict the future consequences of their actions—for example, where promises are not kept and rules are not enforced consistently—then they will learn that acting impulsively—grabbing the small reward now—is the smart thing to do.

Playing a Game That Requires Self-Control

What We Saw

During free-play time, several children start an impromptu game of Duck, Duck, Goose! Marco runs around randomly and refuses to sit down when his turn is done. Leshawn says to Marco, "If you're doing that, you are not playing our game!" Marco then begins playing properly. Within a few minutes nine children are playing Duck, Duck, Goose!

What It Means

A child who, like Marco, runs around aimlessly and doesn't follow the rules will be prone to behavior problems and have difficulty succeeding in school. He needs to learn self-regulation. A game like Duck, Duck, Goose! is well suited to teaching self-regulation because children must control when they run and when they sit, no matter how excited they become. The wonderful thing about this observation is that the children organized the game themselves and then used peer pressure to control Marco. To retain his friends' approval, Marco is willing to exert effort to control his own excitement. Research confirms that children who spend more time at complex social play with peers have a greater ability to self-regulate.[106] Duck, Duck, Goose! is more than just play!

Much of the impulsiveness in young children comes when their attention is captured by a goal that arouses them emotionally and they lack specific skills for calming themselves. Recall the example from the beginning of the chapter. Many of the children were so excited about going outside that they forgot the need to wait in line, and instead ran around the room. Noah, however, was able to wait quietly at the door. How did he do this? He knew that by keeping his back to the door, he could keep his attention off the playground.

Most young children are unable to come up with strategies for distraction. But adults can teach young children distraction strategies that increase their ability to delay gratification.[107] In one study, researchers looked at strategies mothers taught their four-year-old children to help them delay gratification.[108] For the delay task, researchers asked the mothers to teach their child how to wait for a brightly wrapped present sitting in front of them on the table. The child was not supposed to touch the present at all, even when left alone in the room. The mothers could teach their child any strategy. They focused the child on the demands of the task ("Don't touch it. Wait until I come back . . ."), behavioral distraction ("Look at the mirror and make funny faces, or sing your favorite song . . ."), and cognitive distraction ("Think about your favorite TV show . . ."). The researchers recorded how many times each strategy was taught by one of the mothers.

After the teaching session, the child was left alone in the room for five minutes, and the researchers secretly observed whether or not she touched the present. Results showed that most of the children who touched the gift were taught strategies that focused on the demands of the task ("Don't touch it while I'm gone"). In contrast, the children who resisted touching the gift were taught how to distract themselves with an alternate activity or by thinking about something else. Recall our story of Noah waiting in line to go outside: he distracted himself with song. Smart Noah!

ARRANGE THE SETTING TO INCREASE CHILDREN'S RESPONSIBILITY

Over a century ago, Maria Montessori, the famous early educator, started creating special materials for the early childhood classroom that would allow children to take more responsibility for themselves. For example, she used very small pitchers so children could pour milk on their own and very small scissors so they could cut paper on their own. In dozens of other ways, she arranged the environment so children could be more in charge of themselves. Montessori was the first to use this technique.

Teachers today can ensure that their classroom materials—including puzzles, blocks, and books and perhaps paper, glue, and scissors too—are readily accessible to the children without help from adults.[109] To avoid overwhelming small children with too much responsibility—usually indicated by a very messy classroom—many teachers make only a few toys, materials, and tools accessible at first, increasing access each week.

Another way to teach responsibility is to create signs that show where each material is stored. For example, a piece of colored paper (cut in the exact shape of a wooden block) can be taped to the shelf where all blocks are stored. A plastic place mat showing the shapes of a plate, cup, and utensils can help young children when first learning to set the table for lunch. Such aids make learning responsibility much easier. And when children learn the correct way to use or store materials, they are learning to apply a plan to their actions.

Emotional Self-Regulation

Emotions are powerful. They provide both direction and energy to our lives, telling us what we care about and how strongly we care. Compared to behavioral and cognitive self-regulation, dealing with emotions presents different challenges for both children and the adults who care for them.

How Emotional Self-Regulation Develops

Babies can become so overcome by their emotions—crying, thrashing about, gasping for breath—that they have no interest in anything else. All you can do is soothe them until they regain some equilibrium. Over time, most of us learn to cope when we are blocked from achieving a desired action. This is called *frustration tolerance*. Eventually we learn to channel our frustration into problem-solving behavior.

Infants instinctively try to protect themselves from excess stimulation. During their first three months of life, you can see them trying, sometimes successfully, to moderate their arousal. For example, a baby will grow increasingly excited playing peekaboo and then suddenly look away and ignore you for a minute. She is protecting herself by turning away (the infant version of what Noah did while waiting to play outside). Infants also protect themselves by sucking on their thumbs. At around three months infants begin to exercise more voluntary control over their arousal, for example, by breaking eye contact with a caregiver to calm themselves.

While infants have some instinctual ways of dealing with their emotions, they often need help from their caregivers. Whenever they have a need they cannot meet on their own, infants cry to enlist help. By calming and soothing babies before they become overly aroused, we can help them avoid crying episodes. This is good practice, because overly aroused babies often cry themselves to exhaustion—no fun for anyone—and it doesn't help them learn self-regulation. As babies come to trust a caregiver, they begin to calm more quickly and easily (see chapter 1 on attachment).

MISTAKEN PRACTICE

Misuse of Time-Outs

What We Saw

A frustrated child throws a puzzle on the floor and is told to go sit in the time-out chair until she is ready to play again.

Why It Doesn't Work in the Long Run

Sometimes a time-out is exactly what the child needs. But overusing it can interfere with a chance to learn self-regulation. Time-outs as punishment or distraction don't teach a child appropriate ways to manage anger or frustration.

What Would Work Better

Describing the situation in words often helps a child understand what happened. Acknowledging her emotions can help her control them. Using these techniques immediately can diffuse the situation without requiring the child's removal from the area.

Talk with the child calmly. Gently touch her shoulder or hold her in your lap. "You're trying so hard! You're *frustrated* because you can't get the pieces to fit." Give her time to identify the emotion, rather than trying to ignore it. Teach the child coping skills. "Take a deep breath. Now, would you like me to help you try again?" Some practitioners call this approach "time-in" to regain control.

Toddlers learn additional ways to calm their emotions.[110] When they grow frustrated, some can *substitute a new goal.* For example, when Kara runs to the painting easels only to find them occupied, she can handle her frustration if she can think of another activity she enjoys, such as the classroom computer.

Toddlers also use *self-talk* to calm and control themselves. For example, you may observe a child repeating to herself, "Don't run, don't run," as she walks quickly across the room. Self-talk can be used to offer self-encouragement, but it's most often used by a child who is having trouble controlling impulsiveness. It's a means to control one's emotional arousal. As tasks become more difficult, children use more self-talk. Self-talk is one of the ways improved language and cognitive skills help toddlers regulate emotions.[111] It leads to better attention and better performance on challenging tasks.[112]

Preschoolers begin to learn other methods of emotional control. For example, some can use *cognitive reframing*—changing their interpretation—to find something good about a bad situation. "I didn't get my turn, but I get to be first next time."[113]

By the time they reach preschool, children differ greatly in their ability to regulate their emotional responses. Fortunately, teachers can take advantage of their increasing social, emotional, and cognitive skills to help them learn how to regulate their emotions more effectively.

Researchers have found that some preschool-aged children believe that their emotions are somewhat controllable. This belief is called *emotional self-efficacy*, a kind of self-fulfilling prophecy. When you believe you can manage your emotions, you are more likely to do so.[114]

Emotion Recognition

Once children have language, emotional competence can take a huge leap forward. The skills involved are so simple that we sometimes take them for granted: the ability to recognize and label one's own emotions and the emotions of others. This domain of learning is crucial in early childhood programs, and it's a type of learning that teachers can readily promote.[115]

Learning to recognize one's emotions is much easier when teachers provide children with a vocabulary of feeling words. When a child learns a feeling word by having it matched to his current experience, he gains a new emotional understanding. Whereas children start their understanding of emotions with three basic emotions—sad, mad, and glad (happy)—adults can distinguish hundreds of different emotions.

TEACHING CHILDREN TO RECOGNIZE FACIAL EMOTIONS

Many children's books focus on feelings. Teachers can help children learn about them by using dialogic reading, that is, interrupting the reading to ask questions about the story: "How does Marta feel now?" or "Look at Raji's face. What does he feel?" The same methods can be used with puppets and fingerplays.

Some teachers display pictures of people with different facial expressions. Children are encouraged to name what the person is feeling.

When children can label a feeling, they can make the leap from unconscious experience to conscious control. Maria Montessori first wrote on this topic. (Child psychologist Jean Piaget later borrowed the notion from Montessori.) She believed that children first learn things concretely, through experience. After enough experience, they learn the same thing at the next level: abstractly. For example, young children will go to the playhouse and playact an argument they saw that morning between family members. They will enact it over and over again, playing each of the characters in order to understand it concretely, through experience. When they are older, however, children won't need to reenact the situation because they will have the abstract ability to imagine what each person was feeling. Similarly, a child may need to count on her fingers until she truly understands the concept of numbers.

Learning the word for an emotion is not a concrete but rather an abstract, conceptual learning. The word "angry," for example, is a label that can be used over and over again to identify when the same feeling is experienced. The word allows a child to recognize the feeling more consistently and to recall earlier experiences with it. In this way he learns from experience and begins taking conscious control of his emotional expression.

When children can use words to express themselves, they have less need to act out their feelings. They can use their words, for example, instead of their fists.

TEMPERAMENT AFFECTS SELF-REGULATION

Some of the inborn traits of temperament can influence how a child deals with difficult emotions such as frustration. Three of these traits are:

- Intensity of reaction: the strength or loudness of a child's reactions. For example, when hungry, does he fuss or howl?
- Sensitivity: the level or threshold of stimulation—sounds, lights, touch, or smells—needed to get a reaction from a child. Does she wake from napping when the phone rings or sleep through a thunderstorm?
- Adaptability: the ease with which a child gets used to anything new, including transitions (to and from napping) and intrusions (being picked up or helped with a coat).

When working with a child who has intense reactions, especially high or low sensitivity or limited adaptability, exceptional patience and understanding are required. Keep in mind that the loudness of a child's voice may not correspond to his emotional state. Use a soft voice and gentle touch with a highly sensitive child; move deliberately to avoid startling him. For a child who is less adaptable, routines and foreshadowing may ease transitions. Using words to describe the situation and the child's feelings may also help. Describing the situation can help the child reflect on himself—a higher brain activity—and he can then move beyond the immediate emotional response.

Emotional Expression

Children must learn to regulate themselves when frustrated or angry. But they must learn to regulate their positive emotions too. Glee is okay at the park, but probably not at the hospital. Early care and education programs are especially good environments for learning when and where different types of emotion are appropriate. The setting presents many different social situations for learning appropriate ways to express emotion.

Keep in mind, however, that the display of emotions differs among families and cultures. A boy who talks loudly and excitedly, with lots of hand gestures and body movement, may simply be expressing emotion in the manner appropriate to his family or culture. Teachers have the challenging task of respecting these expressions while simultaneously teaching the child to adjust his emotions when faced with particular situations.

Further Reading

On Research

Bronson, M. B. 2000. *Self-regulation in early childhood*. New York: The Guilford Press.

On Practice

Bronson, M. B. 2000. Recognizing and supporting the development of self-regulation in young children. *Young Children* 55 (2): 32–37.

Gillespie, L. G., and N. L. Seibel. 2006. Self-regulation: A cornerstone of early childhood development. *Young Children* 61 (4): 34–39.

Children's Books

Bang, M. 1999. *When Sophie gets angry—really, really angry*. New York: Blue Sky Press.

Carlson, N. 1996. *Sit still*. New York: Viking.

Cresswel, H. 1987. *Trouble*. New York: E. P. Dutton.

Curtis, J. L. 2004. *It's hard to be five: Learning how to work my control panel*. New York: Joanna Cotler Books.

Fox, M. 2000. *Harriet, you'll drive me wild!* Hong Kong: Harcourt, Inc.

Freymann, S., and J. Elffers. 1999. *How are you peeling? Foods with moods*. New York: Arthur A. Levine Books.

Henkes, K. 1996. *Lilly's purple plastic purse*. New York: Greenwillow Books.

Horowitz, D. 2005. *Soon, baboon, soon*. New York: G. P. Putnam's Sons.

Josse, B. M. 1989. *Dinah's mad, bad wishes*. New York: Harper & Row.

Keats, E. J. 1967. *Peter's chair*. New York: Viking Penguin Books.

Moss, M. 1990. *Regina's big mistake*. Boston: Houghton Mifflin Books.

Munsch, R. 1985. *Thomas' snowsuit*. Toronto: Annick Press, Ltd.

Rockwell, A. 1995. *No! No! No!* New York: Macmillan Books for Young Readers.

Sendak, M. 1963. *Where the wild things are.* New York: Harper and Row.

Shannon, D. 1998. *No, David!* New York: Scholastic Inc.

Viorst, J. 1972. *Alexander and the terrible, horrible, no good, very bad day.* New York: Macmillan Publishing Co.

Wells, R. 1997. *Noisy Nora.* New York: Dial.

~~~~~~

When Teachers Reflect: *Can Self-Discipline Replace Discipline?*

Suppose you wanted to make sure the children in your class were well behaved by the end of the year. This means they could follow the directions of future teachers even when excited. One way to approach this goal is through guidance and discipline. You would make classroom rules clear and enforce them consistently. This is certainly a good idea.

But one of the most useful things you could do may come as a surprise: play Red Rover or Red Light, Green Light every day. Or sing "B-I-N-G-O" every day or two, and challenge children to restrain themselves from singing the omitted letters. These traditional songs and games are perfect for teaching impulse control.

If you did one of these activities every day for the first two months of the year, every child would have a chance to learn how to control her impulses and become thoughtful in the course of action. Your class would become better behaved.

You could then move on to more difficult aspects of self-regulation, such as planning one's activities and delaying gratification in working toward a goal.

Once again, the science of child development is finding good justification for some of the most traditional, old-fashioned "nursery school" practices. On the one hand we have fancy technical terms like "development of self-regulation" and "impulse inhibition," and on the other hand we have "Red rover, red rover, let *blue* come over!"

Is it possible that teaching self-regulation could replace child discipline? What is the right balance of each at the beginning of the year, and what is the right balance at the end of the year?

~~~~~~

When Teachers Reflect: *Self-Regulation and Creativity*

Impulsive children often have difficulty with open-ended materials such as clay or paints and may try to avoid them. Children at the painting easel, for example, must impose their own plans onto the materials, which impulsive children find difficult to do. To be creative, a child must impose his own plan onto the materials.

There is a bit of an irony here. The toys that require the most creativity from children are usually the plainest of materials: blocks, paints, clay. The toys with bright lights, electric sounds, and moving parts are often the ones that actually allow the least creativity by the child.

Impulsive children are drawn to toys that structure their experience for them, but as their teacher you need to slowly move them to toys and materials that require more creativity from the child and less from the toymaker!

List six toys or activities in your early childhood program, starting with the one that provides the most structure and ending with the one that provides the least structure (the one that requires the child to do most of the structuring). If you observed the children in the classroom using these toys or activities, could you use your list to rate how self-regulating each child is?

~~~~~~

When Teachers Reflect: Attention-Deficit/Hyperactivity Disorder

You can't study impulsiveness without thinking about children diagnosed with attention-deficit/hyperactivity disorder (ADHD). These children are unable to inhibit their activities on command, they seem incapable of controlling the speed of their responses, and they exhibit restless movement. Many psychologists argue that the issue is less hyperactivity than inability to control attention and behavior. Children with ADHD seem highly active because they lack behavioral organization.

Physicians and psychologists often have difficulty diagnosing ADHD because many preschoolers are normally fidgety and impulsive. In fact, researchers have yet to invent a test for ADHD that works reliably for children under age four.[116] Because it is a diagnosis, ADHD is a yes/no decision; the child is said either to have it or not. But there is a more useful approach for educators, especially during the early childhood years. Think of ADHD along a continuum. Instead of a child either having or not having ADHD, think of the abilities needed to regulate one's attention and behaviors as a set of skills that *all* children have to a greater or lesser degree. The good news is that we can help all children increase their ability to control and plan their own behavior.

Some children need to be referred to a physician and will benefit from medical attention. But in the meantime, as an educator, you are probably best off treating an impulsive child as having a delay in the development of normal self-regulatory abilities. You can teach a child impulse control, frustration tolerance, reflective problem solving, orientation toward the future, and delayed gratification.

Letter to Parents

Did You Know?
Learning self-control doesn't come naturally to children. They must learn it.

Did You Know?
Children who have more self-control as preschoolers are better liked by other children and get better grades when they enter school.

Did You Know?
Our child care program teaches children self-control every day.

We Teach Self-Control in Ways That Might Surprise You
When we play games like Red Light, Green Light or Freeze Tag, or sing the "B-I-N-G-O" song, we are helping your child learn to control his impulses, to think before acting. These aren't just fun games and songs; they are challenging tasks that develop your child's ability to regulate her behavior.

When children are frustrated and we help them think through a problem, we are teaching them *frustration tolerance* and *reflective problem solving*.

When we help children break down a big job into little parts and talk about how we got the big job done, we are teaching them how to accomplish big things through *self-organization*.

Our Program Teaches Children How to . . .

- control their impulses
- tolerate frustration
- organize

. . . a little at a time, every day.

We are a child care program, but we also provide *early childhood education*. Let us know how we are doing!

4

Why We Keep a Pot of Coffee
Family-Centered Care and Education

A father arrives to drop off his infant daughter, Nyssa. Teacher Renee chats with the dad while taking off Nyssa's coat, asking how she slept last night and about her mood this morning. The father replies that Nyssa was a little fussy while eating this morning. Renee thanks the father for the information and tells him she'll keep that in mind during the day. Renee also tells the father they will be taking a walk today to look at the flowering tree in the park. When the father kisses Nyssa and begins to leave, Teacher Renee squats by her on the floor and says, "Say, 'Bye-bye, Daddy!'" Since Nyssa is playing on the floor with a toy, Renee picks her up and shows her that Dad is by the door. Nyssa looks at her father with a smile. As he leaves, Renee says, "Have a good day."

Teacher Renee has built a good relationship with Nyssa's father, who seems as comfortable as his daughter is with the morning ritual. The teacher promotes two-way sharing of information about the child, which is essential for good care. She makes sure the child acknowledges the parent's departure, so there is predictability to the daily separation from the parent. In the months ahead, Nyssa will very likely go through a phase of increased separation anxiety, but well-established arrival and departure routines will contribute to smoother transitions and less anxiety for everyone.

What Is Family-Centered Care?

When a child is passed from one set of arms to another, it is easy to see that (a) children live in multiple social worlds and (b) the early care and education program is in partnership with the family. But during the rest of the day, when the family is not present, the social world of the child and the teacher-caregiver shrinks to the size of their room. The teacher may come to view children as if they exist only within that classroom, or as if the classroom is the center of the child's world. Of course, the child certainly doesn't see the situation this way! When children enter the classroom, they bring with them their family relationships and cultures. We might not always see those family relationships and cultures, but they are always a key part of the child's mental and emotional life.

 *Practice Tip*

How Do We Begin to Build Family-Centered Care?

Starting small is okay. Begin by making sure that each parent is greeted personally during drop-off and pickup times. Child care teachers always greet the children, but we sometimes forget to include the parents. Be sure to say the names of the children and their parents correctly. Ask the parent if you are unsure of a pronunciation. If greeting the parents feels unnatural at first (or if the parents do not respond with an equally welcoming greeting), remember that you are a professional and that building a bond with a parent whose child is in your care is good for the child and lays the foundation for future communication. Over time, your exchange with the parents will relax and warm up.

In recent decades one of the biggest changes in the field of early care and education has been the development of a partnership with the family and the community to promote children's development. The shift has not been easy; in fact, it has barely begun in many programs. Most people entering the early childhood field do so because they love working with children, not because they love working with adults. We are patient when young children make mistakes, but not so patient when their parents make them. We are skilled at working with children, but less prepared to work with their parents.

During this time, researchers have been charting the ways early care and education programs can improve partnerships with families, partnerships that, in turn, improve child development. The first three chapters of this book showed how caregivers and teachers improve children's social and emotional development through *direct* interactions. Chapter 4 describes our *indirect* impact on children, by interacting with their parents and by linking them in supportive networks, including the wider community of family support services. "Evolving over the past three decades," writes one scholar, "is the image of early childhood programs as family support systems that function as modern-day versions of the traditional extended family."[117] In this chapter, we review how early childhood programs evolved into the family support role, describe how teachers and parents influence each other, and suggest ways to gradually make programs more family-centered.

 **Practice Tip**

A Family-Friendly Classroom

To make very young children comfortable and accepted, the early childhood classroom should feel like an extension of home. This can be accomplished in a number of ways. In your program you likely have posters, books, and toys that are developmentally appropriate for all the children in your care, including those with special needs. But do your materials also reflect the cultures and ethnic backgrounds of the children? Children and parents should see themselves reflected in the classroom. Ask parents for pictures of family members. Posting them comforts the children and tells the parents they are valued.

The Roots of Family-Centered Practice

The ongoing shift to a more family-centered view of early care and education has been spurred by five influences over the past several decades:

1. Project Head Start, created in the early 1960s, included a strong family component, partly because some policy makers worried that a national early childhood program might

weaken the family's influence on young children. (As we saw in chapter 1, this fear was probably unwarranted.) Head Start programs were mandated to include four kinds of parent involvement: participation in the classrooms, home visits from Head Start staff, educational activities for parents, and decision-making power in the operation of the programs.[118] In addition, many of its programs even had a staff member who worked *only* with parents. Because Head Start was national in scope and trained tens of thousands of early childhood professionals who went on to work in non–Head Start programs (including some of the coauthors of this book), its model of parent involvement has had an impact on the early childhood profession.

2. Early childhood teachers often provided care and early education experiences without considering the variety of family and cultural approaches to adult–child interactions. However, since the 1960s, minority cultures in North America have pushed for recognition and acceptance. Today, the field of early care and education expects everyone to develop multicultural competence. It is a basic social skill that all adults need for success in multicultural workplaces and communities.

Early childhood programs are a great place for children to begin developing these competencies. To promote awareness of cultural differences, early childhood programs introduce elements of families' cultures into their classrooms through books, food, dress-up clothes, posters, songs, and rituals. Many programs have moved beyond multicultural awareness and understanding. They promote an anti-bias curriculum, which uses the cultural differences between enrolled families as an opportunity to teach children not just to accept differences, but to oppose oppression.[119]

 *Practice Tip*

> ## Begin the Conversation by Focusing on Strengths
>
> Early childhood educators have important knowledge to share with parents, but parents may feel intimidated by a professional who knows more than they do about child development. You can ease this anxiety by developing a "strength-based" approach with parents. "Strength-based" means recognizing that all families have strengths and that using these strengths can create the foundation for further learning.
>
> You will need to practice looking for strengths in the child and sharing them with the parents. Each day jot down something the child has done well. Share the success with the child as well as with the parent. This serves two purposes. An objective comment on an activity the child has done successfully helps the child focus on what she did well. Passing along your observations to parents allows them to share in the success. For example, if you note that a child identified three colors today, you might say to her mother, "Maggie pointed out red, green, and blue today. Have you helped her learn this?" In this way, Maggie's mother will feel acknowledged as her child's first and most important teacher, and she will want to talk with you more.

3. Beginning in the 1970s Urie Bronfenbrenner evaluated early childhood programs for the federal government. He found that those with the greatest positive impact on children's development almost always included considerable parent involvement.[120] He speculated that parental involvement might be the key to long-term impact on children, because parents continue to influence their children for many years after the preschool program ends. Bronfenbrenner was the first to suggest that the biggest positive impact on children's development probably occurs in programs that take a two-generation approach, treating both the parent and the child as developing individuals. Since then, the most effective early education programs have included strong parent involvement and parenting education components.[121]

    Direct tests of the effects of parent involvement in early childhood programs have produced mixed results.[122]

However, slowly accumulating research has begun to make clear the value of engaging parents in their children's early childhood programs. Studies have found that when programs and families work in greater partnership, teachers become more sensitive in their interactions with children,[123] and parents become more supportive of their children's learning.[124] In a study of Head Start preschool children that measured how much they learned from fall to spring, the greatest improvements in learning skills and classroom behavior were made by the children with the most involved parents.[125] Very similar findings have been reported for first-grade children, findings in which greater parent involvement predicted better first-grade outcomes, even after adjusting for children's initial level of intellectual readiness for school during kindergarten.[126] In another study, children's educational attainment at age twenty was predicted by both their mothers' and their fathers' involvement in their educational programs when they were seven years old.[127] This finding supports Bronfenbrenner's idea that while early childhood programs influence a child's development for a few years, parents continue to influence the child for many years thereafter. The fact that parental involvement continued to have long-lasting impact on children up to age twenty confirms the importance of working with both parents and children in early care and education settings.

TIPS FOR BUILDING PARTNERSHIPS WITH PARENTS

1. *Discuss your expectations during a pre-enrollment meeting or intake interview.* Pre-enrollment discussions between teachers, directors, and parents help define expectations. Many conflicts occur as a result of parents' or teachers' unmet expectations of each other. Sharing expectations about caregiving approaches and goals increases parent satisfaction with the program and caregiver satisfaction with parents, not to mention the quality of child care. This meeting sets the foundation for trust and understanding between caregiver and parent; it begins the process of sharing important caregiving information about the child.

2. *Take the time to build the relationship.* At arrival and departure times, make the most of opportunities for informal discussions with parents. First, connect with each parent on a personal level, especially the ones who seem reluctant to talk. Ask how the parent is doing and how the child has been. Sometimes a cooperative spirit can be initiated just by calling the parent by name and offering a sincere smile. Second, schedule regular, uninterrupted times to sit down with parents to discuss changes, developments, concerns, and progress. Organize these conferences so they are relaxed, two-way exchanges of information and insight.

3. *Respect and accept parents.* Tension in the caregiver–parent relationship is often the result of the natural protective instinct that both have toward the child. Mistrusting each other's way of providing care is common. When you recognize a negative feeling toward a parent, try to suspend judgment. If you investigate his rationale, you might better understand his practices and beliefs. Keep in mind that parents want to do their best for their child. Your job as an early childhood teacher is to support them in doing so.

4. *Emphasize the positive.* Often, the best way to improve a tense relationship with a parent is to change your viewpoint by reframing. Look for one thing you value about the parent, one thing she does well with her child. Then convey your appreciation. You may feel awkward doing this, but it may still be very helpful. A parent who feels respected rather than judged is in a better position to release her negative feelings and to begin communicating her concerns nondefensively.

4. Social scientists used to study children individually, in the strange environment of the psychology lab. But subsequent research showed the inaccuracy of this approach. For example, findings would show systematic differences based on where the child lived and other influences; sometimes a cause-and-effect relationship would appear in one group of children but not in another. Today scientists have adopted

a new theory of child development, one that takes into account the child's *social ecology*, that is, his family, neighborhood, and culture.[128] To produce accurate research on children, their *social ecology* must be acknowledged. For an early care and education program, the most important parts of children's social ecology are their families and cultures. Unless you learn about them, your view of children will be incomplete.

5. Even before researchers had verified the importance of engaging families in early childhood programs, the early care and education field decided that parent involvement should be a key part of its policies defining high-quality care and education. Since 1984 accreditation by the National Association for the Education of Young Children (NAEYC) has required that each accredited program "[establish and maintain] collaborative relationships with each child's family to foster children's development in all settings." Programs must be "sensitive to family composition, language and culture."[129] NAEYC's widely respected guidelines, *Developmentally Appropriate Practice*, emphasize the positive relationship of parents and teachers.[130] Scientific research supports these policies. According to Ghazvini and Readdick[131] and Roach et al.,[132] programs judged to be of higher quality communicate with parents more.

In summary, the shift toward families has had five influences: (a) the diffusion of new practices (from Head Start); (b) moral arguments about the inclusion of different cultures; (c) research findings on the effectiveness of family-centered programs; (d) new theories that increase the accuracy of understandings about children; and (e) the policy initiatives of professional associations.

In the following sections, we will describe a few of the key research findings and offer ideas on how to improve early childhood programs by strengthening relationships with families. The practical ideas are important, but so are the research studies: they tell us *why* we should do what we do.

In What Way Does Parent Involvement Matter?

Why should a well-developed home–school partnership lead to improved child development? We can think of at least two explanations. Family involvement creates greater consistency between the home environment and the center, and it also contributes to parent education.

Consistency Between Home and Center

Better coordination between teacher and parent increases the consistency of the child's treatment in the two settings. This consistency helps her feel more comfortable so that she can explore more and feel confident in her interactions. Naptime is a simple example. When staff follow a child's naptime routine, as explained by parents—using the bathroom, saying goodnight to a favorite stuffed animal, singing the same quiet song, lying down quietly—the child has an easier time adapting at the early care program. Experiencing consistency in both environments, home and center, promotes a sense of trust, making exploration and learning more likely.

Another example of parent–program coordination is when the staff learns about enrolled families' cultures. The result is a consistency based not on a single family, but on a cultural group. This has important implications. Take autonomy, for example. The fact that cultures differ greatly in how much they value individual autonomy in a child (compared to interdependence with others) could influence whether children are allowed to serve their own food, for example, or use a pacifier when napping at home.

LEARNING CULTURALLY APPROPRIATE PRACTICE

It is tempting to imagine learning about other cultures before you begin working with families in an early care and education program, but the idea is impractical and might be harmful. It is impractical because there is too much to learn; it may be harmful because it could lead to stereotyping. After all, individual members of a culture can differ greatly from each other. The best bet, therefore, is to nurture a sincere interest in families' cultures and remain open to learning from enrolled families.

Besides making programs and families more consistent, parent–program partnerships can also change the parents. For example, parents could learn practical child-rearing skills from the programs—our next topic.

PROMISING PRACTICE

What We Saw

A father stops in to visit his infant son, Mario. Teacher Anna greets the father warmly as she continues to feed Mario. Anna tells the father what Mario did so far that day: he sat up for a while playing, listened to favorite songs, and watched the birds outside the window. The father shares that they are putting Mario on his tummy a little each day at home, and he is pushing up a lot with his arms. Anna finishes feeding Mario, washes his face, and hands him to his father. As the father holds Mario and Anna cleans the countertop, they talk about how exciting it is to watch Mario try new things and about the next developmental milestones.

What It Means

Teacher Anna's friendly greeting and eagerness to chat helps pull this father into a conversation that emphasizes their partnership in caring for Mario. Anna lets the father see how feeding and sanitation routines are handled—like their children, parents learn by observing models—and she answers his questions about development. This kind of time spent together—sharing information informally about the child—helps ensure consistency of care for Mario and helps the father feel comfortable about the quality of that care. Teacher Anna gains information about Mario's experiences at home and about the parents' child-rearing practices and goals. The partnership of parent and provider creates benefits for parent, child, and caregiver.

Parent Education

Recent research findings have confirmed that parents learn a great deal about child rearing from their early care and education programs. In a study of children from low-income households, researchers looked at the quality of their child care settings as well as how much intellectual stimulation children were receiving at home.[133] Two observations were made, with one year between them. The researchers found that some homes became much more intellectually stimulating during the school year and that these were the homes of children attending higher quality child care programs. Researchers inferred that parents adopted the activities and ways of interacting they encountered at the child care program.

This is consistent with findings of another study[134] in which parents were asked whether they had learned anything from their child care provider that helped them become a better parent. Most parents answered yes. When the same question was asked of the seventy-five child care providers in the study, 79 percent gave examples of ways they knew they had helped parents learn about child rearing. Both parents and child care providers saw informal "parenting education" taking place in the child care setting.

Most of the parents' responses fit into one of the following five categories; some of their responses are given below.

1. Learning to encourage a child's independence
   - "I have a tendency to do too much for my child. Provider has encouraged me to let child do more for herself, even if it takes longer."
   - "I realized that my son can be a good helper in the kitchen instead of a nuisance."

2. Getting emotional support as a parent
   - Learning "to relax more about certain things and to keep my sense of humor."
   - "My provider and I have become like friends. I can listen to her and she to me. That's nice."

3. Learning through role modeling
   - "Most importantly, I get to watch her relaxed, warm, firm, fun behavior with the other children."
   - "[I learned] when not to worry about toilet training! Her relaxed attitude has helped me to relax."

4. Learning from the provider's knowledge and expertise
   - "She is a wealth of knowledge at each stage of my child's development. She's helping us with methods to deal effectively with two-year-old behavior."
   - "She knows a lot about nutrition and feeding strategies, routine medical issues, and general baby well-being. I like her advice because, unlike my mom and sister, she doesn't have an agenda."

5. Learning activities parents can do at home
   - "[She has taught me] things to do with my son for fun and learning."

- "[I've gotten] good ideas on activities to do with our child at home."

PARENT-FRIENDLY EARLY LEARNING

The following advice on creating a good relationship with parents is adapted from *Parent-Friendly Early Learning*[135] by Julie Powers:

1. Be available. This could mean just taking a few moments during arrivals and departures to talk with the parent about her day or her child's day. If you are comfortable talking about everyday things, parents will feel more comfortable coming to you when they have a serious concern.
2. Follow their lead. Let parents lead the conversation as much as you can. You will learn more about their hopes and concerns, and they will feel your respect.
3. Be yourself, within professional boundaries. If you share information about yourself, parents will feel more permission to share information about themselves. This is how every relationship builds. You do not have to become their friend, and in fact you may prefer a more formal relationship. But it is still good for parents to see you as a real person.
4. Show that you are trustworthy. As you develop relationships with families and learn more about them, show them you can be trusted with personal information. Avoid sharing news about one family with another without first getting permission.
5. Create a trusting relationship. A trusting relationship makes tough discussions work better. Telling a parent something difficult about his child is very hard and likely to result in a defensive response unless you have first built a trusting relationship.

Caregivers in this study recognized their active role in the teacher–parent partnership. They reported knowing they were being watched by parents, and that they were teaching parents about child rearing by modeling best practices. Caregivers anticipated inquiries about common parenting concerns such as toilet training, hitting and aggression, sleep disturbances, and separation anxiety. Many providers handed out articles on these topics to interested parents.

In addition to parenting practices, communication about child health issues was an important aspect of the partnership. Providers were asked whether they had been first to notice a child's medical problem or illness, or the first to respond to a serious accident. Almost two-thirds (65 percent) answered yes. The most common response was that they had spotted the early (or sometimes advanced) symptoms of an ear infection. "I often know when the day care children are sick before the parents do," said one respondent. Many providers also wrote about times they served as a health screening and referral service. In other words, they were the first professional who brought a problem to the parent's attention and encouraged referral to a health professional. One teacher noted that an infant wasn't developing physically, and indeed, at three and a half months of age the child was diagnosed with Infant Muscular Dystrophy. Another teacher correctly read a child's symptoms as yeast infection when the parent assumed mere diaper rash. Finally, a caregiver explained how she took pains to assure the parent that though she was not an expert and could be wrong, she was concerned about an apparent speech impediment. Based on the sensitive way the message was delivered, the child soon got tested.

 *Practice Tip*

> ## What About the Difficult Parent?
>
> Some parents seem to ignore all attempts at communication. If you send home a newsletter, you find it days later in the child's backpack. If you call, you get a number that is no longer in service. When you greet them, you barely get a nod. How do you engage these parents?
>
> First, do not give up. As is the case with challenging children, sometimes it is the challenging parents who most need our resources and attention. Avoid assuming you are not liked or appreciated. Sometimes stress in the family creates almost insurmountable obstacles so that day-to-day concerns about the early care and education program are neglected. Try to remain upbeat. Try different ways of communicating. Send the newsletter, but post it in the classroom as well. Ask another parent to volunteer to greet parents and share information. Ask the difficult parent if she has time to stay for ten minutes and chat with you. You might preface the invitation by explaining that she seems very busy and you just want to get to know her a little better. Isolated parents may be unused to positive adult interaction, and more effort will be needed to build trust.

These research studies lead to some unexpected and important conclusions. First, early care and education programs appear to be having a significant, and largely unseen, effect on the quality of child rearing in this country. These programs may be the largest and most effective system of parenting education in the United States! Of course, early childhood staff don't see themselves primarily as parent educators. Very few have a book of ideas and materials to use with parents. This is a type of expertise that the early childhood field is just beginning to recognize and support.

The finding on health screening is also interesting. Just as early care and education programs may be the most widespread and effective form of parenting education in the country, they may also be its most extensive health-screening system. Both of these conclusions are possible because most American children are in child care today. Prior to entering school, early care and education programs have daily contact with more families than any other modern American institution.

TRY THIS!

We visited a part-day preschool program that requires parents to attend several trainings per year. The parents agree to this as part of the enrollment contract. One training gave an overview of the state early learning standards (see chapter 5) and how the program philosophy of "learning through play" was supported by the standards and by developmentally appropriate practices. Parents commented that the training helped them to understand how their children were learning and why it was important to preserve play in the early childhood years!

It is not surprising, then, that the U.S. organizations specializing in preventing child abuse are so interested in working with early care and education programs. (For example, visit the Strengthening Families project at www.cssp.org/doris_duke/index.html.) Just as early childhood educators can spot the early signs of ear infections or speech delays, they can spot the early signs of child maltreatment. If we want to help parents learn enough about child rearing to avoid maltreatment, once again, early childhood educators are situated better than anyone else to provide that knowledge. This is true because:

◆ Early childhood teachers often see parents daily, and a solid relationship can form over time. Within this relationship, parents can observe natural, nonthreatening adult–child interactions in a convenient setting, just as they might have done when extended families were common.

◆ Early childhood teachers and caregivers have legitimacy as experts on child development, and parents respect them. This is much more relevant because of today's small families. About half of the children in early childhood programs are first-borns—and they are being raised by first-time parents. In contrast, program staff typically have helped raise many children over time. They understand common developmental patterns and variations.

◆ Since early childhood staff tend to be approachable, parents can discuss their concerns more easily than with many other professionals.

For these reasons, no other group of professionals is likely to be better situated to improve the quality of parenting in modern society.

Many programs recognize this fact and offer parenting education classes to enrolled families. But as we've already seen, parents can learn quite a bit from informal interactions. In fact, some parents avoid parenting education because it implies they lack knowledge or skills. This is why parent–program partnerships are now considered a better approach. In a partnership, both parents and teachers have strengths to contribute. Parents can learn a lot from each other.

FAMILY-CENTERED CARE IS DIFFERENT FROM PARENT INVOLVEMENT

Family-centered care reframes the goal of early care and education programs. Instead of promoting the care and development of the child directly, the goal is to bring together the mutual expertise of both families and early care programs for the benefit of the child. According to Keyser,[136] family-centered care has five essential characteristics:

1. The program and the family recognize and respect one another's knowledge and expertise.
2. Information is shared through two-way communication.
3. Power and decision-making are shared.
4. The program acknowledges and respects diversity.
5. The program helps create networks of support for families.

Social Support for Parenting

Besides providing greater consistency between center and home, and supporting parent education, family-centered programs also provide opportunities for parents to learn from each other. Observing and talking with other parents, especially those they know well and see often (a social network of peer parents), is actually one of the main ways parents all over the world learn to be better parents.

Parents have always had help raising their children, most often from extended families, neighbors, friends, and their communities. Today, we add the early childhood educator—a new and increasingly important part of parents' social support networks. Early care and education programs enable parents to meet other parents with children the same age. The social support networks that result can be very helpful to families.

The social network is crucial because no single parent has all the knowledge and skill that a group or community of parents can offer. The trick is to find ways for parents to connect with each other, so they can learn what others know, see how others handle children, and get practical help when needed.

It should come as no surprise, then, that hundreds of research studies have found that parenting competence and child development are better, by all metrics, when parents have more sources of social support: more people to talk to about parenting, more people to count on for assistance in a pinch, more people with whom they feel a sense of community.[137] For example, when parents have more social support, they are more likely to form secure attachments with their infants.[138]

HOW CAN WE GAIN GREATER INVOLVEMENT BY FATHERS?

One study found three surprisingly simple actions that led to greater involvement by fathers in early care and education programs:[139]

1. Include the father's name on the enrollment form.
2. Send letters from the program to the father as well as the mother, even if the father lives apart from the child.
3. Invite fathers to participate in activities at the center.

Indeed, one of the most consistent predictors of a child-abusing family is social isolation—no neighborhood picnics, no friends over for dinner, no community involvement.[140] This is true of all human societies. We tend to raise our young well when integrated into healthy communities, but poorly when isolated from others.

But why does social support have such a positive impact? According to research, social support is not just one influence, but a rich mixture.[141]

◆ Observational learning. Parents can learn from other adults interacting with children. They might see how a child care provider gets the children to put away the blocks, or observe another parent's method of easing their child through the end-of-the-day transition.

- Child-rearing advice. Parents can ask others for advice. Of a teacher they may ask, "How do you get her to try new foods?" Of a parent they might ask, "How did you toilet train your son?" or "What do you do when your son talks back to you?"

- Information exchange and referral to community resources. Parents learn from others without even having to ask: a friend tells them about a library story hour, or a newsletter alerts them to a free immunization clinic.

- Social control of the parents. Communities not only teach and support, but limit or control as well. Every community has norms: some behaviors are okay and others are forbidden. This is one reason why socially isolated parents tend to maltreat their children: there is no outsider to observe the maltreatment and step forward to say, "Hey, you shouldn't shake a baby. You could hurt him."

Practice Tip

Working with Teen Parents

Working with teen parents takes patience above all else. Adolescence is partially defined by egocentric behavior, and teen parents find themselves balancing the desire for a social life against the responsibilities of parenthood. For the child care teacher, this means working essentially with two children, infant and adolescent.

Building trust with a teen parent—who may be pushing away his own parents in striving for independence—is critical. But trusting another adult, even his child's caregiver, is difficult. Listen to the teen parent and show your respect. Teens are likely to shut down if they feel judged. Once trust is earned, keep your advice short and simple.

Remember that peers (other teenagers) are important to teens, but they may not have the parenting skills or experience to be a resource.

Like many teenagers, teen parents can be forgetful and disorganized. They may need many reminders to do seemingly obvious things such as bring food or clothing for their child. With a teen parent, however, you have the chance to become a trusted resource and make a real difference.

- ◆ Child care exchange. In friendly, well-functioning communities, parents keep an eye on each other's children, feeding them when they are hungry, making sure they are safe. Shared caregiving gives each parent a break from the burden of continuous caregiving. Participants can share babysitting in the evening, trade off driving the children to the early care program, and help each other with emergency child care when needed.
- ◆ Social valuing of the parental role. When parents are valued for their everyday efforts, they may feel better about themselves in general and have greater motivation to do their best. When a neighbor stops by to visit a new baby and expresses joy while holding her and gazing into her eyes, the neighbor is telling the parent: "You have done something wonderful in producing this beautiful child. Your work as a parent is important to everyone." This feeling that their "work" is valued

by the community can make a big difference in how parents view themselves and how carefully they perform their role as parents.

◆ Emotional support as a person. Every parent has an independent adult life. If they are lonely or anxious or depressed, they may be less effective as a parent. When a teacher asks a father about his wife's health, the topic is not parenting, but the emotional connection can make the father stronger as a person and thus a better parent. When two mothers lean against the play yard fence at the end of the day, talking about a new job or about the possibility of getting their families together for dinner that weekend, they are creating mutual, emotional support.

All of these social supports can be provided by early education teachers. The idea is to help the parent learn to be a better parent and to deepen the relationship between parent and teacher. The deepening of this relationship has further effects. For example, if the teacher needs to talk with the parent about a difficult issue (e.g. their child's misbehavior or health concerns), a strong relationship makes the discussion much easier.

 *Practice Tip*

Defining the Family

Let the parents take the lead when it comes to defining their families. A child may live in two homes or in foster care, have same-sex parents, or be raised by other relatives. Your intent is to make the child welcome in your program by embracing her family. The more you know about who touches the child's life, the better you can understand, support, and educate that child.

Ask parents where the child spends time outside of school and who is important in the child's life. Consider having a "getting to know you" event to meet with parents and find out more about them. Be sure to introduce yourself to anyone who drops off or picks up the child to make them feel welcome. When the children are old enough, have them draw pictures or tell stories about all the people they know. Every glimpse into the lives of the children gives you greater insight into ways to support their social and emotional development.

Parents can give each other social support too. Early care and education programs help parents build their own networks of friendship and mutual support. The center is the place where parents can meet and form long-lasting relationships. In fact, we might say that relationships among enrolled families create community, and that child rearing is easier and better within it.

 *Practice Tip*

If You Feed Them, They Will Come!

Consider a family lunch or dinner at your program. Eating together can ease social anxiety for parents who do not know each other. If you group the parents by their children's ages, there is some common ground for conversation. You could offer an educational component, explaining to parents how children learn through play, or the importance of reading. If you decide to convene these gatherings on a regular basis, ask the parents about topics of interest. Look for guest speakers when the topic is outside your expertise. Giving parents a social outlet gives them a chance to build social supports.

Fostering Community Connections

The social support networks among parents in your program are one kind of community. There is also the community of agencies and organizations beyond the program whose services affect families and child development. The early care and education program has a role to play in creating connections between these programs and enrolled families.

Early care and education programs have begun to serve the broader needs of families, beyond their child care needs, because serving those broader needs promotes both the parent's and the child's development. Until their basic housing and food needs are met, and until they feel safe, most parents will have a difficult time getting involved in their child's early care and education program or improving their child-rearing methods. Basic needs come first. Therefore, to help the child's development, many programs today are finding ways to improve the family's overall situation.

For example, some early childhood programs colocate with other community services (housing assistance, employment, and health and nutrition programs such as WIC). Once the staffs get to know each other, early childhood staff can readily introduce parents to other service providers. Even when programs do not colocate, familiarity with other community programs helps early childhood staff guide families to other services.[142]

Using Community Resources

What We Saw

As parents and children arrive in the morning, they are greeted by a nutritionist from the county extension office who hands out warm muffins. The parents also get a recipe card and information on nutrition programs offered by the extension office.

What It Means

What could be more welcoming than freshly baked muffins? This treat was easy to arrange because the extension office was looking for ways to reach out to parents of young children. Both organizations, the early care and education program and the extension office, benefited from working together.

Community programs, such as those provided by the public health department, are sometimes willing to bring their services directly to the early childhood program as part of their outreach efforts. When screening for hearing, vision, or developmental delays; free immunization; or WIC sign-up is brought right to the center, parents are far more likely to take part. The services are not only more convenient but are provided in a setting parents already trust.

Barriers to Family-Centered Practice

Although shifting from child-centered programs to family-centered programs makes good sense, it is not easy to accomplish. At least three kinds of barriers stand in the way.

Lack of Staff Training in Working with Parents and Families

Early childhood teachers and caregivers differ greatly in how much formal training they have received. But whatever the training, its focus is almost exclusively on the child. Families may not show up on the radar. This makes sense: providers enter the field to work with children, not parents and families.[143] Although inadequate training is common, as over half acknowledged in one study,[144] even limited training could make a difference in helping early childhood staff shift to a more family-centered role.

Staff Attitudes toward Parents

Studies over the past quarter century have consistently found that many early childhood teachers hold a negative attitude about parents' child-rearing skill and effort.[145] Even in a study of family-focused programs, many staff judged parents harshly, believing children got too little care and attention from them.[146] While all parents love their children and want the best for them, not every parent is as skilled as early childhood staff. Because early childhood teachers and caregivers dedicate their working lives to nurturing young children, we should not be surprised when they judge parents by their own high standards.

This attitude of staff toward parents is a concern. According to one study, when early childhood staff held a low opinion of a particular parent, they spoke much less to her.[147] The irony in this finding is that the parents who appeared to need the most assistance from the program were those receiving the least contact with it. After reviewing the findings on this topic, one researcher warned that early childhood teachers may see themselves as saviors or "surrogate parents and try to assume more responsibility for the child than is appropriate or desired by the parent."[148] A better strategy is to see the parent (as well as the child) as a developing individual. Early childhood teachers are very good at building on young children's strengths; they are patient when teaching them new skills. Might they use the same patience and understanding when working with the parents in learning new skills?

If early childhood teachers and care providers see parents as developing individuals and as people who love their children and want the best for them, it will be easier to respect them and adopt a helpful attitude toward them. Such an approach is really just an extension of the way providers work with children.

MISTAKEN PRACTICE

Parent Bashing

What We Saw

Teacher 1 (from the staff lounge): "I can't believe Dad brought in Sean after I sent him home sick yesterday."

Teacher 2: "At least he picked him up yesterday. I have a parent who never comes when I call. I think she cares more about her job than her child!"

Why It Doesn't Work

Negative attitudes can interfere with effective communication between teacher and parent. If the parent senses disapproval, she may be less inclined to comply with future requests. Other results may include loss of trust and damage to the program's effectiveness.

Why It Happens

First, teachers genuinely care about the children in their programs; if they feel protective of the child, there may be tension in the teacher–parent relationship. Second, the teacher's needs may oppose those of the parent. For example, the teacher may claim, "I want to keep the other children from getting sick," or "I don't have enough time to care for a sick child who needs so much attention." The parent, on the other hand, may say, "I can't leave work again to care for my sick child. I might get fired." While teachers need a place to vent their frustrations, doing so with other staff can create a hostile environment for both parents and children.

What Would Work Better

When dealing with conflict, reflect on the parent's perspective. Instead of merely complaining to colleagues, ask about the validity of your feelings and reactions. (Am I overreacting? Why does the parent act this way?) Consider how your experiences and attitudes may influence your reaction.

Think, too, about how effectively you are communicating with the family. Keep the lines of communication open and clarify policies and expectations. Can you see the issue from the family's perspective? ("I know it's hard to leave work when your child is suddenly sick. You're pulled in different directions with work and family responsibilities.") Help families with information so they get the assistance they need. ("Here's the number of a program that cares for mildly ill children. Perhaps they can help.") Meanwhile, make sure you are managing your own stress and getting the support and resources you need in your classroom.

Family Resources and Challenges

No matter how much we adapt our programs to focus them on the family, family involvement will be limited. This is because no matter how much parents and other caregivers "love their children, understand child development, or sincerely want to become involved, [they] are frequently faced with too little time," whether two-income or low-income households.[149] On the bright side, most parents of young children want more information on helping their children learn.[150] They want the expertise that early care and education programs can provide.

 *Practice Tip*

When a Child Care Teacher Is Not a Parent

If you are an early education teacher who is not a parent, be prepared for parents to question your ability to give advice. If you anticipate questions, you can have answers ready. If you keep your goal in mind—partnering with parents—you'll have an easier time. Here are some responses to doubting parents. Consider saying, "You are the expert on your child. All I can tell you is what seems to work for other families." This statement recognizes that parents know best what works with their child and you know what works with most children. While parents are interested in your knowledge, they need to know that they get to decide what to do with their own child.

Another strategy is to agree with the parent and then carve out an area of common interest. You might say, "You're right: I don't have children of my own. I'm very thankful for the chance to get to know the children in this class. Could I ask you about something? Let me share with you something your daughter did today, and see if you've seen the same thing at home."

Sometimes a parent might challenge you because he fears you know more about children or have greater skill with them than he does. He might even fear the close relationship you have with his child. This can be especially true for first-time parents. If a parent fears that you are taking over their role, you can empathize and communicate respect, which will undercut a feeling of competition by focusing on your partnership and relationship: "No, I don't have children, and I wonder sometimes how you can work all day and still have the energy to care for this little whirlwind of energy. I know I'm exhausted at the end of the day. How do you do it?"

Don't forget to ask parents for their input. They want affirmation; they want to know that they bring a special expertise to the relationship.

Steps to Promoting Family-Centered Practice

If you wanted to make an early care and education program more family-centered, what would you do first? As noted, providing staff with some training in working with parents and families is a good first step. Not only do staff need new skills, but the training is also a good way to communicate that family-centered practice is expected of them. Second, a similar message needs to be communicated to parents. If they believe that you expect them to be involved, they are more likely to be so.[151] Parents need to develop a sense of confidence or trust in the program before they will become very involved.[152]

How do programs develop that trust? One study examined programs that were making a real effort to increase their parent involvement. The results suggested that fostering deeper parent involvement might be a two-step process.[153] Consistent with the idea that trust comes first, the study found that parents need to have an initial feeling of warmth about an early childhood program, a feeling of being welcome and respected as an essential first step before any other family involvement would follow. The programs in the study created comfortable spaces for parents and offered child-rearing books, games, and other resources for parents to use. Having food or a coffee pot handy added to creating an informal, welcoming atmosphere.

PROMISING PRACTICE

Children Teaching the Parents

What We Saw

Families have come to an open-house night at the center. Parents circulate from one activity area to another, and at each area two children show the parents how to use the materials properly. Some of the areas have brief handouts for the parents. For example, a handout in the block area explains how unit blocks teach the math concepts of sets, ordering, and multiples.

What It Means

Switching roles this way empowers the children (and really impresses the parents). The children rise to the occasion, taking seriously their responsibilities of teaching and monitoring. This kind of open house helps parents understand what and how their children learn. Parents prefer it to learning the same things from teachers.

———

One of the programs in the study held a regular "popcorn and movies night" for the whole neighborhood. When the researchers visited the site, they saw that the "main room [was] crowded with families and buzzing with conversation. Current families [were] enjoying the informal social time while formerly enrolled families [were] thrilled to see familiar faces." The researchers speculated that "new families, when they eventually enroll their children, [would] return with warm feelings, making high levels of involvement in parent-oriented activities much more likely."[154] This event is especially interesting because it was not about child development or early education; it was just a fun family activity taking place in the same building. Nonetheless, it encouraged friendships and social support among parents; friendly relations between parents and staff; and welcoming feelings in the early childhood center that could set the stage for parent participation in their child's education or in programs aimed at the parents themselves.

According to a recent study of all licensed child care programs in one state, nearly three-quarters (72 percent) hosted fun social events (see Table 4.1) for the entire family.[155] An even greater percentage of programs reached out to parents with information, either with an information board on the wall (96 percent) or by regular distribution of a newsletter spotlighting family activities and children's accomplishments at the program (86 percent). Many fewer (44 percent) had a parent center in their facility.

A high percentage of programs also worked on face-to-face interactions with parents. For example, over three-fourths of programs (77 percent) trained their staff to work with families and expected their staff to do so; the same percentage recruited family members as volunteers in the program. Fully 90 percent of programs in the study held a conference with each family at least once per year to discuss the child's progress.

A much smaller percentage of programs pioneered more intensive forms of family engagement. Typically these were Head Start programs (whose funding requires such forms of family services) and nationally accredited programs. Over one-quarter (28 percent) of all programs in the state offered regular educational workshops for families, and 20 percent had a staff member dedicated to working directly with families.

Table 4.1 **Percentage of Early Care and Education Programs Offering Family-Centered Practices**

Family-centered practices	Programs (%)
Provide an information board for families	96%
Hold conferences with families at least yearly	90%
Publish regular newsletter featuring children and families	86%
Recruit family members as volunteers	77%
Train staff to work with families	77%
Regularly host social events for the entire family	72%
Provide a family resource center and free parent resources	44%
Sponsor regular educational workshops for families	28%
Dedicate a staff member to working directly with parents and families	20%
Provide annual home visits with each child and family	13%

Source: M. A. Roach, Y. Kim, D. B. Adams, D. A. Riley, and D. Edie. 2006. How can we strengthen families through early care and education? *Wisconsin Child Care Research Partnership, Issue Brief no. 17, 2.* Madison: University of Wisconsin–Extension.

PROMISING PRACTICE

What We Saw

A computer-generated note, complete with border, is posted on the parents' bulletin board. It describes what the children did in the classroom that day and includes digital photographs of children engaged in activities. Each day a new note is posted; previous notes are placed in a three-ring binder below the bulletin board. Browsing the binder, parents get a snapshot of what happens in the classroom each day.

What It Means

When parents ask their children what they did all day, the answer is often "Nothing!" These posted pictures and descriptions of the classroom's daily activities gave parents enough information to start conversations both with teachers and with their own children ("I saw you went to the library today. Can you tell me about it?"). It also let parents know that the teachers in this classroom carefully plan and organize their activities.

These results show the kinds of formal activities programs offer, such as educational workshops and social events. Yet they tell us nothing about the informal interactions between parents and staff, which might be even more important in the development of a relationship between parent and teacher. For example, every day drop-off and pickup times provide opportunities for face-to-face communication between staff and parents. Researchers have been interested in how well these times are used by programs and whether they make a difference. One study of sixteen child care centers found that about two-thirds of transition times involved staff-parent communication, although this figure differed greatly from one program to another.[156] In one center, staff and parents did not communicate at all about half the time. In another center, staff initiated conversation with parents during 76 percent of opportunities.

What did they talk about in these transition-time conversations? About half were more than just routine greetings. Most included asking for or giving information about the child's behavior (like the observation that began this chapter), the child's or adult's health, or the child's day at the center. These conversations were usually brief, typically lasting only about twelve seconds. But twelve seconds can create continuity in the child's care and trust in the parent–teacher relationship.

Not surprisingly, programs with greater parent–teacher communication are rated as providing higher-quality care.[157]

MISTAKEN PRACTICE

From Savior to Shared Care

Many teachers go through an evolution in how they think about their relationships with parents.[158] When they begin working with parents, many have a "savior complex" and feel they can save children from the poor parenting techniques of their fathers and mothers. Hopefully, these teachers soon see the arrogance and naïveté of this perspective. Or teachers may come to see parents as clients. In this view, the teachers are experts, and the job of parents is to listen and follow advice. While teachers may be experts on children in general, parents are the experts on their own child.

We suggest that the most successful teachers see parents as partners in caregiving. The teacher's role is seen as supplementing and supporting parents, not substituting for them. Parents who work with such teachers feel respected and supported, and remain open to learning from them.

_____

In Summary

Good programs provide opportunities for children to learn while their parents work. Great programs go further by strengthening families. Such programs have:

- Welcoming environments that respect and reflect families' values.
- Multiple opportunities for families to become a part of their children's education.
- Strong communication systems that help build relationships with families and among families.
- Ready connections to other community organizations that serve families.

The influences on child development stretch far beyond the walls of the early care and education program. We see the child embedded within a family system; we see the family within a social network of families and a community of family-support programs. Early care and education programs are just one of these programs, but they are crucial because they teach parents so much about child rearing and work so well helping parents meet other parents and build supportive networks.

As early childhood professionals, we know "that we can have a deeper and more meaningful impact on child development by partnering with the child's family. We can learn from the family how to adapt our program to their values, goals, and culture. Families can learn from us how to continue developmentally appropriate practices at home. And for many families, we can become an advocate that connects them to other beneficial programs in the community."[159]

Further Reading

On Research

Galinsky, E., and B. Weissbourd. 1992. Family-centered child care. In B. Spodek and O. N. Saracho, eds., *Yearbook in early childhood education, Volume 3: Issues in Child Care*, 47–65. New York: Teachers College Press.

Powell, D. R. 1998. Reweaving parents into the fabric of early childhood programs. *Young Children* 53: 60–67.

On Practice

Bradley, J., and P. Kibera. 2007. Closing the gap: Culture and the promotion, of inclusion in child care. In *Spotlight on young children and families*, ed. D. Koralek, 38–42. Washington, D.C.: National Association for the Education of Young Children.

Carter, M. 2001. Changing our attitudes and actions in working with families. *Child Care Information Exchange* 138: 48–51.

Clay, J. W. 2007. Creating safe, just places to learn for children of lesbian and gay parents. In *Spotlight on young children and families*, ed. D. Koralek, 24–27. Washington, D.C.: National Association for the Education of Young Children.

Ferede, K., and E. D. Hou. 2006. The family involvement storybook: A new way to build connections with families. *Young Children* 61 (6): 94–97.

Kaczmarek, L. 2007. A team approach: Supporting families of children with disabilities in inclusive programs. In *Spotlight on young children and families*, ed. D. Koralek, 28–36. Washington, D.C.: National Association for the Education of Young Children.

Keyser, J. 2001. Creating partnerships with families: Problem-solving through communication. *Child Care Information Exchange* 138: 44–47.

Keyser, J. 2006. *From parents to partners: Building a family-centered early childhood program*. St. Paul: Redleaf Press.

Koralek, D., ed. 2007. *Spotlight on young children and families*. Washington, D.C.: National Association for the Education of Young Children.

Powers, J. 2005. *Parent-friendly early learning*. St. Paul: Redleaf Press.

Children's Books

Boon, D. 1998. *My gran*. Brookfield, Conn.: The Millbook Press.

Brown, M. 1947. *Stone soup*. New York: Aladdin Books.

Cooper, M. 1993. *I got a family*. New York: Henry Holt and Company.

Cowen-Fletcher, J. 1994. *It takes a village*. New York: Scholastic.

Dotlich, R. K. 2002. *A family like yours*. Honesdale, Pa.: Boyds Mills Press.

Fox, M. 1997. *Whoever you are*. New York: Harcourt Brace.

Michelson, R. 2006. *Across the alley*. New York: Putnam.

Williams, V. B. 1990. *More more more*. New York: Greenwillow Books.

When Teachers Reflect: Knowing the Parents

1. List the names of the parents of all of the children in your care. Who did you forget? Why?
2. Put yourself in the parents' shoes: list all the feelings you imagine parents feel when they leave their children in your care.
3. List three things about a parent who bothers you or with whom you do not get along.
4. List three things about a parent you like and with whom you get along well.

Simply listing from memory the parents of the children in your group can illuminate gaps in your relationships. Parents you cannot remember are often those with whom you fail to communicate. Perhaps they are uncomfortable talking with you; perhaps they seldom drop off or pick up their child, or show up for conferences. Do you make yourself available at arrival and departure times? Do you greet each parent (and child) by name? Is there some aspect of the program that suggests disapproval of the parents? Can you think of ways to make the program more welcoming for this family?

Consider the feelings of parents, and what they are telling themselves, when they leave their children in your care:

- Worry (Will my child be okay?)
- Anxiety (Is this the best place for my child?)
- Fear (What if something bad happens?)
- Guilt (I'm a bad parent for leaving my child.)
- Sadness and loss (What milestones might I miss?)
- Jealousy (Will my child love you more than me?)
- Relief (I need a break.)
- Contentment (I'm so glad I found this great program for my daughter.)

Recognizing the emotions that parents experience can help you understand and communicate more effectively. The parent who lashes out over a child's lost sweater may be anxious about his child's well-being (If you can't keep track of my child's sweater, how can you keep my child safe and well?). Rather than react defensively, you may be able to address the underlying fear.

Reflecting on your own responses to parents can give you

insight into the attitudes and biases rooted in your past—either in childhood relationships or your experience as a parent. Perhaps a parent reminds you of a disapproving grandmother, or a parent's personality brings back memories of a squabble with a sibling. By recognizing your own reaction and the basis of that reaction you set aside your emotional response and can deal more objectively with the situation at hand.

***

When Teachers Reflect: *Lessons from Research on Families with School-Age Children*

Joyce Epstein, the preeminent authority on family–school partnerships during the elementary and middle-school years, has summarized the six key ways in which families and schools create fruitful partnerships.[160] Some are important for parents, some for children, and some for the school. There is no guarantee that her findings from families with older, school-aged children will make sense for the early childhood years, but we might learn something by asking. The six types of involvement are:

1. Parenting support: Helping parents learn more about child development, parenting, and the kinds of behavior they should expect of their children at home.
2. Communicating: Finding ways to keep the parents up-to-date on the activities at the school.
3. Volunteering: Finding ways to recruit parents to help at the school or attend school functions.
4. Learning at home: Suggesting learning activities that parents can do with their children at home. Epstein found that this form of parent involvement had the biggest impact on children's development.
5. Decision making: When parents feel they have real power and/or when they feel they are truly being heard when decisions are made, they will feel ownership of the school and find other ways to increase their involvement.
6. Collaborating with the community: The school can take the initiative to connect parents with other community resources.

How could an early childhood program advance each of these forms of parent involvement? For example, how could it promote learning activities for parents at home that relate to their children's learning in the program (item 4)? Or if steps were taken to improve community collaboration (item 6), to what programs might we connect parents?

5

Why We Do What We Do
for Children's Social Development
Explaining Your Program Practices in
Terms of State Early Learning Standards

What Are Early Learning Standards?

Most states are adopting Early Learning Standards to describe
the practices and outcomes expected in early childhood settings.
The implementation of these standards reflects an increasing appreciation by state and national policymakers that experiences
in early childhood settings have a significant influence on future
school success. To explain how your program meets the standards, you must cover not only physical, language, intellectual,
and socio-emotional development, but also how a child "learns
to learn" (in the language of the standards, "approaches to
learning").

The design and implementation of state early learning standards is a fairly new development in the history of the early
care and education field. Although all states have yet to develop them, it seems likely that each state will work toward that
goal. To find out how far individual states have progressed, visit
http://nccic.acf.hhs.gov/pubs/goodstart/elg-efforts.html, or ask
your licensing agency, state department of education, or child
care resource and referral agency.

How Early Learning Standards Create a Common Language

The variety of early learning regulations and requirements can be confusing. For instance, there are Head Start performance standards and public school academic standards; there is also child care licensing. Early learning standards provide a common language when people with different backgrounds and educational levels are working together in the best interest of young children and families. Many community collaborations use their state's early learning standards to provide a shared understanding and framework for their work with children and families. The standards can be used to unite all partners around best practices in early care and education.

Using Early Learning Standards

Early learning standards are not meant as a curriculum or assessment tool. Rather, they are designed as a shared framework for understanding and communicating expectations about young children's development. Many state early learning standards align with curricula such as the High/Scope® curriculum and the Creative Curriculum®. For programs that do not use a formal curriculum, early learning standards can form part of the teaching cycle by bringing consistency to the planning, implementation, and assessment of children's programming.

Early childhood professionals must be prepared to describe how their program meets state early learning standards in their curriculum, environments, and interactions with children. Although the standards are broken down into domains, they merge and overlap in practice. The categories are not intended to be rigid. For example, when facilitating children's outdoor play, teachers may observe large-muscle skill development, small-muscle manipulation, self-regulation behaviors, social skills, language development, and cognitive-processing skills. All this happens while children play together in a sandbox or take turns going down a slide! A single activity may contribute to many performance standards.

Must classroom environments and activities change to meet the early learning standards? Perhaps not. Most high-quality programs already provide programming that meets the intent of these standards. The bigger challenge, largely unmet by the early childhood profession, is in *communicating* developmentally appropriate practice and programming to other adults.

Communicating with parents about your program helps them understand *why* you do *what* you do. Many parents do not understand that, in early childhood, every moment is a teachable moment. The vast majority of learning is based on the child's own self-motivated actions along with our helping the child to reflect on those actions, not through worksheets, memorization, or group lessons. As a professional you will need to teach parents and others how children learn every day through routines, purposeful activities, and interactions with a carefully constructed environment. You will also need to explain how the best early childhood settings look very different from later schooling environments. Here is where the language of your state's early learning standards can help you interpret for them your program's philosophy, objectives, and strategies.

Table 5.1 on pages 134–38 lists the early learning standards of two states, Wisconsin and California, in the category of Social and Emotional Development. Next to each standard are two columns: "What you do" and "How and why it meets these standards." Each of these two columns lists information and suggestions in three areas: interactions, environment, and curriculum.

Additional Resources

The charts in this chapter give standards for two states, but you may want to compare them to your own state's standards. This could be a productive activity for a staff meeting or community collaboration.

To find your state's early learning standards, visit http://nccic.acf.hhs .gov/pubs/goodstart/elg-efforts.html, or ask your licensing agency, state department of education, or child care resource and referral agency.

The full set of Wisconsin Model Early Learning Standards can be found at: http://www.collaboratingpartners.com/EarlyLS_docs.htm.

The California PreK Learning Guidelines Desired Results can be found at: http://www.cde.ca.gov/sp/cd/ci/desiredresults.asp.

For a full copy of the California PreK Learning Standards, visit http://www.cde.ca.gov/sp/cd/re/prekcontents.asp.

The NAEYC Position

The National Association for the Education of Young Children (NAEYC) has a position statement on school readiness. When we refer to school readiness for young children, we are talking not only about children being ready for school experiences after the early childhood years, but also about the responsiveness of families and communities to the children and the receptiveness of schools. This is a more encompassing view of what it takes to foster successful learning. To learn more about school readiness, you can visit the National Association for the Education of Young Children website at http://www.naeyc.org/ece/critical/readiness.asp.

Careers in Early Care and Education

Wisconsin has assembled a career guide on the many types of positions in the early care and education profession. Visit http://www.collaborat ingpartners.com/career_g/index.html. Find out if your state has a similar guide. You may be surprised at the employment options.

Further Reading

Gronlund, G. 2006. *Making Early Learning Standards Come Alive: Connecting Your Practice and Curriculum to State Guidelines*. St. Paul: Redleaf Press.

Table 5.1 **Explaining Your Practices in Terms of State Early Learning Standards**

Social and Emotional Development: Emotional Development

Wisconsin Early Learning Standards	California PreK Learning Guidelines	What you do	How and why it meets these standards
• Expressing a wide range of emotions in a variety of settings. • Seeking adult interaction as needed for emotional support, physical assistance, social interactions, and approval. • Self-control. • Use of words to communicate emotions. • Understanding and responding to others' emotions.	Child Desired Results 1, Indicator 3: Children demonstrate effective self-regulation of their behavior. Theme: Self-regulation (impulse control, ability to calm himself or herself, participation in routines, and decision making). Child Desired Result 1, Indicator 2: Children demonstrate effective social and interpersonal skills. Theme: Interactions with adults (social referencing, having a secure base, recognizing the familiar/unfamiliar, and seeking adults for help).	**Interactions** • Acknowledge children's feelings. ("You seem frustrated that you can't ride the tricycle right now.") • Give children words to express emotions appropriately. ("Tell Sara that you really like the red tricycle and would like a turn soon.")	• By acknowledging children's feelings, you teach the importance of listening to others and you acknowledge that having a variety of feelings is okay. • Giving specific words for feelings helps children learn to identify and label what they are feeling.
		Environment • Provide at least two copies of favorite toys or objects in the classroom. • Arrange your classroom so that children have personal space and a place for their belongings. Put children's names on their personal space areas.	• By providing more than one copy of a popular item, more children can use it to comfort themselves, and you encourage the development of turn-taking skills. • Children feel safe, secure, and valued when you recognize that they need personal space just like adults.
		Curriculum • Read books about people and animals who express different emotions in a variety of situations. • Use puppets, dolls, and pictures to show children how to express emotions appropriately.	In order for children to learn in any environment, they need consistent relationships with caregivers. When we help children understand themselves and how to get along with others, we provide a foundation for further learning.

Table 5.1 continued

SOCIAL AND EMOTIONAL DEVELOPMENT: SELF-CONCEPT

Wisconsin Early Learning Standards	California PreK Learning Guidelines	What you do	How and why it meets these standards
• Self-esteem. • Self-direction in choices and actions. • Self-awareness, including abilities, characteristics, and preferences. • Creative self-expression. • Willingness to make needs known and to trust others. • Views self as a teacher/learner.	Child Desired Result 1, Indicator 2: Children demonstrate effective social and interpersonal skills. Theme: Self-concept (independence: development in knowing and valuing self; growing ability to make independent decisions and choices). Child Desired Result 1, Indicator 1: Children show self-awareness and a positive self-concept. Theme: Self-awareness (dependence and interdependence: understanding that one's self is a separate being with an identity of his or her own and with connectedness to others).	**Interactions** • Greet children with their names each day and show sincere interest and joy at seeing them. • Talk positively about what children are doing and learning. • When a child accomplishes something that stretches his learning, comment on it. (Examples: Infant: "You worked really hard to reach that bear, and now you can feel how soft it is!" Toddler: "You used red, yellow, and green on your paper and made it very colorful!" Preschooler: "You helped Sara get the red ball. That was a very nice thing to do".	• Developing relationships with the children you see every day is crucial to their self-esteem. • There is a difference between praise and encouragement. Praise does not always provide a direct connection between what the child has done and why it matters, e.g., "Good job!" • Encouragement helps children see that what they did made a difference, either to themselves or to someone else. It helps children become aware of themselves and their actions. Magda Gerber calls teachers who use this type of talk with children "broadcasters" or "announcers."
		Continued on page 136.	

Table 5.1 continued

SOCIAL AND EMOTIONAL DEVELOPMENT: SELF-CONCEPT

		What you do	How and why it meets these standards
		Environment	
		• Display children's pictures and artwork at their level. • Provide a variety of developmentally appropriate materials on low, open, and labeled shelves. • Make sure the environment has pictures, materials, and books that represent all of the children's cultures and lifestyles.	• When children see that we value them and their work, they feel better about themselves. The impact is even greater when we emphasize the process over the product. • When children can choose materials that are age-appropriate and return them with minimal assistance, they are learning self-awareness about their environment.
		Curriculum	
		• Honor every child and family by sharing family pictures and traditions in the classroom. • Plan ways to help children express their uniqueness through music, movement, art, or nature exploration.	• Every family has unique traditions and backgrounds. Recognizing them and asking families to share helps each child feel good about herself. • When you give children different ways to express themselves, you help them access their creativity and ultimately help them discover themselves.

Table 5.1 continued

SOCIAL AND EMOTIONAL DEVELOPMENT: SELF-CONCEPT

Wisconsin Early Learning Standards	California PreK Learning Guidelines	What you do	How and why it meets these standards
Interacting with one or more other children. • Seeking out peers as play partners. • Participating successfully as a member of a group. • Using words and other positive strategies to resolve conflicts. • Understanding when and how to ask for adult help.	Child Desired Result 1, Indicator 2: Children demonstrate effective social and interpersonal skills. Theme: Interaction with peers (social interaction, friendship, empathy, participation in groups, cooperation, and negotiation). Child Desired Result 1, Indicator 5: Children show growing abilities in communication and language. Theme: Language comprehension (understanding the meaning of information, ideas, and feelings expressed by others; vocabulary development). Child Desired Result 1, Indicator 3: Children demonstrate effective self-regulation of their behavior. Theme: Self-regulation (impulse control, ability to calm himself or herself, participation in routines, and decision making).	**Interactions** • Greet children, parents, and coworkers with respect. • Model problem-solving behaviors such as taking turns, negotiation, sharing, and consensus. • Act as a play facilitator to help children learn social skills throughout the day. **Environment** • Set up the classroom with interest centers that promote small-group interaction of children. • Arrange the classroom to avoid overcrowding in popular areas. • Add or change materials based upon the interests of children. • Display pictures of children playing together.	• Children watch and listen to us at a very early age. When we model positive interactions, we are more likely to see children display positive behavior. • The ultimate goal is to teach children how to solve their own problems. When we model a variety of techniques to rectify a situation, we are helping children learn positive strategies for social competence. • When we set up interest areas for reading, puzzles, sensory activities, and block building, we are creating mini-environments where children can work and play with each other. • When we pay close attention to the classroom environment, we are setting the stage for greater social competence.
		Continued on page 138.	

Table 5.1 continued

SOCIAL AND EMOTIONAL DEVELOPMENT: SELF-CONCEPT

		What you do	How and why it meets these standards
		Curriculum	
		• Read stories with themes of social interaction and friendship. • Create routines and transitions that emphasize working together and getting along. • To encourage social skills, play games such as cooperative musical chairs, Parachute Play, and Ring Around the Rosie.	• At all ages we can read books to children about friendship, asking for help when needed, and solving conflicts. As children absorb the concepts, they become more likely to practice the strategies in social situations. • Routines and transitions are very important aspects of early care and education programs. You will be saving time and integrating "teachable moments" if you use them to promote social skills. • Using games to teach social skills has been a long tradition in education. With young children it makes sense to have fun while you learn!

Notes

1. Grossman, K. E., K. Grossman, and P. Zimmerman. 1999. Attachment relationships in the context of multiple caregivers. In *Handbook of attachment: Theory, research, and clinical applications,* edited by J. Cassidy and P. R. Shaver, 760–786. New York: The Guilford Press.

2. Jacobsen, T., W. Edelstein, and V. Hofman. 1994. A longitudinal study of the relation between representations of attachment in childhood and cognitive functioning in childhood and adolescence. *Development Psychology* 30:112–124.

3. Weinraub, M., and M. Lewis. 1977. The determinants of children's responses to separation. *Monographs of the Society for Research in Child Development* 42 (4):1–78.

4. Howes, C. 1999. Attachment relationships in the context of multiple caregivers. In *Handbook of attachment: Theory, research, and clinical applications,* edited by J. Cassidy and P. R. Shaver, 671–687. New York: The Guilford Press; Schaffer, H. R., and P. E. Emerson. 1964. The development of social attachments in infancy. *Monographs of the Society for Research in Child Development* 29 (3):1–77.

5. Schaffer, H. R. 1996. *Social development*, 131. Oxford: Blackwell Publishers.

6. Honig, A. S. 2002. *Secure relationships: Nurturing infant/toddler attachment in early care settings*, xiii. Washington, D.C.: National Association for the Education of Young Children.

7. Hazan, C., and P. Shaver. 1987. Romantic love conceptualized as an attachment process. *Journal of Personality and Social Psychology* 52:511–524.

8. Ainsworth, M. D. S., S. M. Bell, and D. J. Stayton. 1972. Individual differences in the development of some attachment behaviors. *Merrill-Palmer Quarterly* 18:123–143.

9. Urban, J., E. Carlson, B. Egeland, and L. A. Sroufe. 1991. Patterns of individual adaptation across childhood. *Development and Psychopathology* 3:445–460.

10. Dozier, M., K. C. Stovall, and K. E. Albus. 1999. Attachment and psychopathology in adulthood. In *Handbook of attachment: Theory, research, and clinical applications*, edited by J. Cassidy and P. R. Shaver, 497–519. New York: The Guilford Press.

11. Howes, C. 1999. Attachment relationships in the context of multiple caregivers. In *Handbook of attachment: Theory, research, and clinical applications*, edited by J. Cassidy and P. R. Shaver, 671–687. New York: The Guilford Press.

12. Goosens, F. A., and M. H. van IJzendoorn. 1990. Quality of infants' attachments to professional caregivers: Relation to infant-parent attachment and day-care characteristics. *Child Development* 61:832–837.

13. Londerville, S., and M. Main. 1981. Security of attachment, compliance, and maternal training methods in the second year of life. *Child Development* 17:289–299.

14. Londerville, S., and M. Main. 1981. Security of attachment, compliance, and maternal training methods in the second year of life. *Child Development* 17:289–299.

15. Park, K. A., and E. Waters. 1989. Security of attachment and preschool friendships. *Child Development* 60:1076–1081.

16. Howes, C., C. E. Hamilton, and C. C. Matheson. 1994. Children's relationships with peers: Differential associations with aspects of the teacher–child relationship. *Child Development* 65:253–263.

17. Howes, C., C. E. Hamilton, and L. C. Phillipsen. 1998. Stability and continuity of child-caregiver and child-peer relationships. *Child Development* 69:418–426.

18. Howes, C., and S. Ritchie. 2002. *A matter of trust: Connecting teachers and learners and the early childhood classroom*, 20–21. New York: Teachers College Press.

19. Sroufe, L. A., B. Egeland, and E. A. Carlson. 1999. One social world: The integrated development of parent–child and peer relationships. In *Relationships as developmental contexts*, edited by W. A. Collins and B. Laursen, 241–261. Mahwah, N.J.: Lawrence Erlbaum Associates.

20. Feeney, J. A., and P. Noller. 1990. Attachment style as a predictor of adult romantic relationships. *Journal of Personality and Social Psychology* 58:281–291; Roisman, G. I., S. D. Madsen, K. H. Hennighausen, L. A. Sroufe, and W. A. Collins. 2001. The coherence of dyadic behavior across parent–child and romantic relationships as mediated by the internalized representation of experience. *Attachment and Human Development* 3:156–172.

21. Bretherton, I. 1985. Attachment theory: Retrospect and prospect. *Monographs of the Society for Research in Child Development* 50:3–35; Sroufe, L. A., and J. Fleeson. 1986. Attachment and the construction of relationships. In *Relationships and development*, edited by W. W. Hartup and Z. Rubin, 57–71. Hillsdale, N.J.: Lawrence Erlbaum Associates.

22. Schaffer, H. R., and P. E. Emerson. 1964. The development of social attachments in infancy. *Monographs of the Society for Research in Child Development* 29 (3):1–77.

23. Parke, R. D., and R. O'Neil. 1999. Social relationships across contexts: family-peer linkages. In *Relationships as Developmental Contexts*, edited by W. A. Collins and B. Laursen, 211–240. Mahwah, N.J.: Lawrence Erlbaum Associates.

24. Honig, A. S. 2002. *Secure relationships: Nurturing infant/toddler attachment in early care settings*, 62. Washington, D.C.: National Association for the Education of Young Children.

25. Shonkoff, J. P., and D. A. Phillips, eds. 2000. *From neurons to neighborhoods: The science of early childhood development.* Washington, D.C.: National Academy Press.

26. Shaffer, D. R. 1994. *Social and personality development*, 3rd ed. Pacific Grove, CA: Brooks/Cole Publishing Company; Brazelton, T. B., B. Koslowski, and M. Main. 1974. The origins of reciprocity: The early mother–infant interaction. In *The effect of the infant on its caregiver,* edited by M. Lewis and L. Rosenbaum, 49–76. New York: Wiley.

27. van den Boom, D. C. 1994. The influence of temperament and mothering on attachment and exploration: An experimental manipulation of sensitive responsiveness among lower-class mothers with irritable infants. *Child Development* 65:1457–1477.

28. Ainsworth, M. D. S., M. C. Blehar, E. Waters, and S. Wall, eds. 1978. *Patterns of attachment*. Hillsdale, N.J.: Lawrence Erlbaum Associates; Isabella, R. A. 1998. Origins of attachment: The role of context, duration, frequency of observation, and infant age

in measuring maternal behavior. *Journal of Social and Personal Relationships* 15:538–554.

29. Adams, D., M. R. Roach, D. Riley, and D. Edie. 2001. Who stays in the early childhood field? State policies can help reduce turnover. *Wisconsin Child Care Research Partnership, Issue Brief #2*. Madison: University of Wisconsin–Extension.

30. Raikes, H. 1996. A secure base for babies: Applying attachment concepts to the infant care setting. *Young Children* 51:59–67.

31. Howes, C., and C. E. Hamilton. 1992. Children's relationships with caregivers: Mothers and child care teachers. *Child Development* 63: 859–866.

32. Ahnert, L., M. Pinquart, and M. E. Lamb. 2006. Security of children's relationships with nonparental care providers: A meta-analysis. *Child Development* 74:664–679; Goosens, F. A., and M. H. van IJzendoorn. 1990. Quality of infants' attachments to professional caregivers: Relation to infant–parent attachment and day-care characteristics. *Child Development* 61:832–837.

33. Barnas, M.V., and E. M. Cummings. 1997. Caregiver stability and toddlers' attachment-related behaviors towards caregivers in day care. *Infant Behavior and Development* 17:141–147.

34. McKim, M. K., K. M. Cramer, B. Stuart, and D. L. O'Connor. 1999. Infant care decisions and attachment security: The Canadian transition to child care study. *Canadian Journal of Behavioural Science* 32:92–106.

35. Vaughn, B., B. Egeland, L.A. Sroufe, and E. Waters. 1979. Individual differences in infant–mother attachment at twelve and eighteen months: Stability and change in families under stress. *Child Development* 50:971–975.

36. Howes, C., C. C. Matheson, and C. E. Hamilton. 1994. Maternal, teacher, and child care history correlates of children's relationships with peers. *Child Development* 65:264–273.

37. Kagan, J. 1976. Emergent themes in human development. *American Psychologist* 64:186–196.

38. Gray, H. 2004. "You go away and come back": Supporting separations and reunions in an infant/toddler classroom. *Young Children* 59:100–107.

39. Belsky, J., and M. J. Rovine. 1988. Nonmaternal care in the first year of life and the security of infant–parent attachment. *Child*

Development 59:157–167; Belsky, J. 1990. Developmental risks associated with infant day care: Attachment insecurity, noncompliance, and aggression? In *Psychosocial Issues in Day Care*, edited by S. Chehrazi, 37–68. New York: American Psychiatric Press.

40. Farran, D. C., and C. T. Ramey. 1977. Infant day care and attachment behaviors toward mothers and teachers. *Child Development* 48:1112–1116; Fox, N. 1977. Attachment of kibbutz infants to mother and metapelet. *Child Development* 48:1228–1239.

41. NICHD Early Child Care Research Network. 1997. The effects of infant child care on infant–mother attachment security: Results of the NICHD study of early child care. *Child Development* 68:860–879; NICHD Early Child Care Research Network. 2001. Child care and family predictors of preschool attachment and stability from infancy. *Developmental Psychology* 37:847–862.

42. Farran, D. C., and C. T. Ramey. 1977. Infant day care and attachment behaviors toward mothers and teachers. *Child Development* 48:1112–1116.

43. Bronfenbrenner, U. 1981. Children and families: 1984? *Society* 18 (2):38–41.

44. Bowlby, J. 1980. *Loss: Sadness and depression.* Vol. 3 of *Attachment and loss.* New York: Basic Books.

45. Bukowski, W. M., and L. K. Sippola. 1996. Friendship and morality: (How) are they related? In *The company they keep: Friendships in childhood and adolescence*, edited by W. M. Bukowski, A. F. Newcomb, and W. W. Hartup, 238–261. New York: Cambridge University Press.

46. Sroufe, L. A., B. Egeland, and E. A. Carlson. 1999. One social world: The integrated development of parent–child and peer relationships. In *Relationships as Developmental Contexts*, edited by W. A. Collins and B. Laursen, 241–261. Mahwah, N.J.: Lawrence Erlbaum Associates.

47. Amidon, E., and C. B. Hoffman. 1965. Can teachers help the socially rejected? *The Elementary School Journal* 66:149–154; Bonney, M. E. 1971. Assessment efforts to aid socially isolated elementary school pupils. *Journal of Educational Research* 64:345–364.

48. Parker, J. G., and S. R. Asher. 1987. Peer relations and later personal adjustment: Are low-accepted children at risk? *Psychological Bulletin* 102:357–389.

49. Roff, M., S. B. Sells, and M. M. Golden. 1972. *Social adjustment and personality adjustment in children.* Minneapolis: University of Minnesota Press.

50. Roff, M. 1961. Childhood social interactions and young adult bad conduct. *Journal of Abnormal and Social Psychology* 63:333–337.

51. Cowen, E., A. Pederson, H. Babigian, L. D. Izzo, and M. A. Trost. 1973. Long-term follow-up of early detected vulnerable children. *Journal of Consulting and Clinical Psychology* 41:438–445.

52. Shaffer, D. R. 1994. *Social and personality development,* 3rd ed. Pacific Grove, Calif.: Brooks/Cole Publishing Company.

53. Howes, C., and C. C. Matheson. 1992. Sequences in the development of competent play with peers: Social and social pretend play. *Developmental Psychology* 28:961–974.

54. Howes, C. 1983. Patterns of friendship. *Child Development* 54:1041–1053; Howes, C., with K. H. Rubin, H. S. Ross, and D. C. French. 1988. Peer interaction of young children. *Monographs of the Society for Research in Child Development* 53 (1):1–92.

55. Park, K. A., K. Lay, and L. Ramsay. 1993. Individual differences and developmental changes in preschoolers' friendships. *Developmental Psychology* 29:264–270.

56. Howes, C., with K. H. Rubin, H. S. Ross, and D. C. French. 1988. Peer interaction of young children. *Monographs of the Society for Research in Child Development* 53 (1):1–92; Ladd, G. 1990. Having friends, keeping friends, making friends, and being liked by peers in the classroom: Predictors of children's early school adjustment? *Child Development* 61:1081–1100; Ladd, G. W., B. J. Kochenderfer, and C. C. Coleman. 1996. Friendship quality as a predictor of young children's early school adjustment. *Child Development* 67:1103–1118.

57. Howes, C., with K. H. Rubin, H. S. Ross, and D. C. French. 1988. Peer interaction of young children. *Monographs of the Society for Research in Child Development* 53 (1):1–92.

58. Park, K. A. 1992. Preschoolers' reactions to loss of a best friend: Developmental trends and individual differences. *Child Study Journal* 22:233–252.

59. Howes, C., with K. H. Rubin, H. S. Ross, and D. C. French. 1988. Peer interaction of young children. *Monographs of the Society for Research in Child Development* 53 (1):1–92.

60. Howes, C., with K. H. Rubin, H. S. Ross, and D. C. French. 1988. Peer interaction of young children. *Monographs of the Society for Research in Child Development* 53 (1):1–92.

61. Hartup, W. W. 1996. Cooperation, close relationships, and cognitive development. In *The company they keep: Friendships in childhood and adolescence,* edited by W. M. Bukowski, A. F. Newcomb, and W. W. Hartup, 213–237. New York: Cambridge University Press.

62. Howes, C., O. Unger, and C. C. Matheson. 1992. *The collaborative construction of pretend: Social pretend functions.* Albany: State University of New York Press.

63. Piaget, J., and B. Inhelder. 1969. *The Psychology of the child.* New York: Basic Books; Sullivan, H. S. 1953. *The interpersonal theory of psychiatry.* New York: Norton.

64. Eisenberg, N., T. Lundy, R. Shell, and K. Roth. 1985. Children's justifications for their adult and peer-directed compliant (prosocial and nonprosocial) behaviors. *Developmental Psychology* 21:325–331.

65. Newcomb, A. F., and C. L. Bagwell. 1995. Children's friendship relations: A meta-analytic review. *Psychological Bulletin* 117:306–347.

66. Hartup, W. W., B. Laursen, M. I. Stewart, and A. Eastensen. 1988. Conflict and friendship relations of young children. *Child Development* 59:1590–1600.

67. Newcomb, A. F., and C. O. Bagwell. 1995. Children's friendship relations: A meta-analytic review. *Psychological Bulletin* 117:306–347; Sroufe, L. A., B. Egeland, and E. A. Carlson. 1999. One social world: The integrated development of parent–child and peer relationships. In *Relationships as developmental contexts,* edited by W. A. Collins and B. Laursen, 241–261. Mahwah, N.J.: Lawrence Erlbaum Associates.

68. Piaget, J. 1977. The coordination of perspectives. In *The Essential Piaget: An interpretive reference and guide,* edited by Howard E. Gruber and J. Jacques Voneche, 621–627. New York: Basic Books.

69. Borke, H. 1975. Piaget's mountains revisited: Changes in the egocentric landscape. *Developmental Psychology* 11:240–243.

70. Teti, D., and K. Ablard. 1989. Security of attachment and infant-sibling relations: A laboratory study. *Child Development* 60:1519–1528.

71. Buysse, V., B. D. Goldman, and M. L. Skinner. 2003. Friendship formation in inclusive early childhood classrooms: What is the teacher's role? *Early Childhood Research Quarterly* 18:485–501.

72. Buysse, V., B. D. Goldman, and M. L. Skinner. 2002. Setting effects on friendship formation among young children with and without disabilities. *Exceptional Children* 68:503–517.

73. Riley, D. 1986. Social interaction and the computer. *Early Childhood Exchange* 8 (3):3–4. Madison: University of Wisconsin-Extension.

74. Roff, M., S. B. Sells, and M. M. Golden. 1972. *Social adjustment and personality adjustment in children.* Minneapolis: University of Minnesota Press.

75. Raver, C., E. K. Blackburn, M. Bancroft, and N. Torp. 1999. Relations between effective emotional self-regulation, attentional control, and low-income preschoolers' social competence with peers. *Early Education and Development* 10:333–350.

76. Parke, R. D., and R. O'Neil. 1999. Social relationships across contexts: Family–peer linkages. In *Relationships as developmental contexts*, edited by W. A. Collins and B. Laursen, 211–240. Mahwah, N.J.: Lawrence Erlbaum Associates.

77. Bretherton, I. 1985. Attachment theory: Retrospect and prospect. *Monographs of the Society for Research in Child Development* 50:3–35; Sroufe, L. A., and J. Fleeson. 1986. Attachment and the construction of relationships. In *Relationships and development,* edited by W. W. Hartup and Z. Rubin, 57–71. Hillsdale, N.J.: Lawrence Erlbaum Associates.

78. Dunn, J., J. Brown, and L. Beardsall. 1991. Family talk about feeling states and children's later understanding of others' emotions. *Developmental Psychology* 27:448–455.

79. Dunn, J., J. Brown, and L. Beardsall. 1991. Family talk about feeling states and children's later understanding of others' emotions. *Developmental Psychology* 27:448–455.

80. Dunn, J., J. Brown, and L. Beardsall. 1991. Family talk about feeling states and children's later understanding of others' emotions. *Developmental Psychology* 27:448-455.

81. Ladd, G., and B. S. Golter. 1988. Parents' management of preschoolers' peer relations: Is it related to children's social competence? *Developmental Psychology* 24:109–117.

82. Kopp, C. B. 1982. Antecedents of self-regulation: A developmental perspective. *Developmental Psychology* 18:199–214.

83. Eisenberg, N., R. A. Fabes, and S. Losoya. 1997. Emotional responding: Regulation, social correlates, and socialization. In *Emotional development and emotional intelligence: Educational implications*, edited by P. Salovey and D. Sluyter, 129–163. New York: Basic Books; Eisenberg, N., and R. A. Fabes. 1998. Prosocial development. In *Social, Emotional, and Personality Development*, vol. 3 of *Handbook of child psychology*, 5th ed., edited by N. Eisenberg and W. Damon, 701–778. New York: John Wiley & Sons, Inc.

84. Campbell, S. B. 1995. Behavior problems in preschool children: A review of recent research. *Journal of Child Psychology and Psychiatry* 36:113–149.

85. Cantwell, D. P., and L. Baker. 1987. Differential diagnoses of hyperactivity. *Journal of Developmental and Behavioral Pediatrics* 8:159–165.

86. Olson, S. L., and B. Hoza. 1993. Preschool development antecedents of conduct problems in children beginning school. *Journal of Clinical Child Psychology* 22:60–67.

87. McLelland, M. M., F. J. Morrison, and D. L. Holmes. 2000. Children at risk for early academic problems: The role of learning-related social skills. *Early Childhood Research Quarterly* 15:307–329; Shoda, Y., W. Mischel, and P. K. Peake. 1990. Predicting adolescent cognitive and self-regulatory competencies from preschool delay of gratification: Identifying diagnostic conditions. *Developmental Psychology* 16:978–986; Mischel, W., Y. Shoda, and P. K. Peake. 1988. The nature of adolescent competencies predicted by preschool delay of gratification. *Journal of Personality and Social Psychology* 54:687–696.

88. Wong, M. M., J. T. Nigg, R. A. Zucker, L. I. Puttler, H. E. Fitzgerald, J. M. Jester, J. M. Glass, and K. Adams. 2006. Behavioral control and resiliency in the onset of alcohol and illicit drug use: A prospective study from preschool to adolescence. *Child Development* 77:1016–1033.

89. Caspi, A., G. H. Elder, and D. J. Bem. 1987. Moving against the world: Life course patterns of explosive children. *Developmental Psychology* 23:308–313.

90. Read, K. H. 1950. *The nursery school: A human relations laboratory*. Philadelphia: W. B. Saunders Co.

91. Elias, C. L., N. Eisenberg, and L. E. Berk. 2002. Self-regulation in young children: Is there a role for socio-dramatic play? *Early Child Research Quarterly* 17:216–238.

92. Heidemann, S., and D. Hewitt, eds. 1992. *Pathways to play: Developing play skills in young children.* St. Paul: Redleaf Press.

93. Maccoby, E. E. 1980. *Social development: Psychological growth and the parent–child relationship.* New York: Harcourt Brace Jovanovich, Inc.

94. Anderson, V. 1998. Assessing executive functions in children: Biological, psychological, and developmental considerations. *Neuropsychological Rehabilitation* 8:319–349.

95. Caspi, A., G. H. Elder, and D. J. Bem. 1987. Moving against the world: Life course patterns of explosive children. *Developmental Psychology* 23:308–313.

96. Kaler, S. R., and C. B. Kopp, eds. 1990. Compliance and comprehension in very young toddlers. *Child Development* 61:1997–2003.

97. Kuczynski, L., and G. Kochanska. 1990. Development of children's noncompliance strategies from toddlerhood to age 5. *Developmental Psychology* 26:398–408.

98. Stumphauzer, J. S. 1972. Increased delay of gratification in young prison inmates through intervention of high-delay peer models. *Journal of Personality and Social Psychology* 21:10–17.

99. McClelland, M. M., F. J. Morrison, and D. L. Holmes. 2000. Children at risk for early academic problems: The role of learning-related social skills. *Early Childhood Research Quarterly* 15:307–329.

100. Maccoby, E. E. 1980. *Social development: Psychological growth and the parent–child relationship.* New York: Harcourt Brace Jovanovich, Inc.

101. Maccoby, E. E., and S. S. Feldman. 1972. Mother-attachment and stranger-reactions in the third year of life. *Monographs of the Society for Research on Child Development* 37:1–86.

102. Kochanska, G., K. Murray, and E. T. Harlan. 2000. Effortful control in early childhood: Continuity and change, antecedents, and implications for social development. *Developmental Psychology* 36:220–232.

103. Hohmann, M., and D. P. Weikart. 2002. *Educating young children: Active learning practices for preschool and child care programs,* 2nd ed. Ypsilanti, Mich.: High/Scope Press.

104. Mischel, W., and E. Staub. 1965. Effects of expectancy on working and waiting for larger rewards. *Journal of Personality and Social Psychology* 2:625–633.

105. Mischel, W., R. Zeiss, and A. Zeiss. 1974. Internal-external control and persistence: Validation and implications of the Stanford Preschool Internal-External Scale. *Journal of Personality and Social Psychology* 29:265–278.

106. Elias, C. L., N. Eisenberg, and L. E. Berk. 2002. Self-regulation in young children: Is there a role for socio-dramatic play? *Early Child Research Quarterly* 17:216–238.

107. Mischel, W., and C. J. Patterson. 1976. Substantive and structural elements of effective plans for self-control. *Journal of Personality and Social Psychology* 54:942–950.

108. Mauro, C. F., and Y. R. Harris. 2000. The influence of maternal child-rearing attitudes and teaching behaviors on preschoolers' delay of gratification. *The Journal of Genetic Psychology* 161:292–306.

109. Bronson, M. B. 2000. *Self-regulation in early childhood: Nature and nurture*. New York: The Guilford Press.

110. Bretherton, I., J. Fritz, C. Zahn-Waxler, and D. Ridgeway. 1986. Learning to talk about emotions: A functionalist perspective. *Child Development*, 55:529–548; Calkins, S., and M. C. Johnson. 1998. Toddler regulation of distress to frustrating events: Temperamental and maternal correlates. *Infant Behavior and Development* 21:379–395.

111. Kopp, C. B. 1982. Antecedents of self-regulation: A developmental perspective. *Developmental Psychology* 18:199–214.

112. Berk, L. E., and S. Landau. 1993. Private speech of learning-disabled and normally achieving children in classroom academic and laboratory contexts. *Child Development* 64:556–571.

113. Harris, P. L. 1993. Understanding emotions. In *Handbook of emotions*, edited by M. Lewis and J. M. Haviland, 237–246. New York: The Guilford Press.

114. Garber, J., N. Braafladt, and J. Zeman. 1991. The regulation of sad affect: An information-processing perspective. In *The development of emotional regulation and dysregulation*, edited by J. Garber and K. A. Dodge, 208–240. New York: Cambridge University Press.

115. Denham, S. A., and R. Burton. 1996. A social-emotional intervention for at-risk 4-year-olds. *Journal of School Psychology* 34:225–245.

116. Lahey, B. B., W. E. Pelham, M. A. Stein, J. Loney, C. Trapani, K. Nugent, H. Kipp, E. Schmidt, S. Lee, M. Cale, E. Gold, C. M. Hartung, E. Willcutt, and B. Baumann. 1998. Validity of DSM-IV attention-deficiti/hyperactivity disorder for younger children. *Journal of the American Academy of Child and Adolescent Psychiatry* 37:695–702.

117. Powell, D. R. 1998. Reweaving parents into the fabric of early childhood programs. *Young Children* 53:60.

118. Zigler, E., and S. Muenchow. 1992. *Head Start: The inside story of America's most successful educational experiment.* New York: Basic Books.

119. Derman-Sparks, L., and the A.B.C. Task Force. 1989. *Anti-bias curriculum: Tools for empowering young children.* Washington, D.C.: National Association for the Education of Young Children; Derman-Sparks, L. 1999. Markers of multicultural/antibias education. *Young Children* 54:43.

120. Bronfenbrenner, U. 1974. *Is early intervention effective? A report on longitudinal evaluations of preschool programs,* vol. 2. Washington, D.C.: Department of Health, Education, and Welfare, Office of Child Development.

121. Ramey, C. T., and S. L. Ramey. 1998. Early intervention and early experience. *American Psychologist* 53:109–120; Yoshikawa, H. 1995. Long-term effects of early childhood programs on social outcomes and delinquency. *The Future of Children* 5:51–75.

122. White, K. R., M. J. Taylor, and V. D. Moss. 1992. Does research support claims about the benefits of involving parents in early intervention programs? *Review of Educational Research* 62:91–125.

123. Ghazvini, A. S., and C. A. Readdick. 1994. Parent–caregiver communication and quality of care in diverse child care settings. *Early Childhood Research Quarterly* 9:207–222.

124. Owen, M. T., A. M. Ware, and B. Barfoot. 2000. Caregiver–mother partnership behavior and the quality of caregiver–child and mother–child interactions. *Early Childhood Research Quarterly* 15:413–428.

125. Taylor, A. R., and S. Machida. 1994. The contribution of parent and peer support to Head Start children's early school adjustment. *Early Childhood Research Quarterly* 9:387–405.

126. Reynolds, A. 1989. A structural model of first-grade outcomes for an urban, low socioeconomic status, minority population. *Journal of Educational Psychology* 81:594–603.

127. Flouri, E., and A. Buchanan. 2004. Early father's and mother's involvement and child's later educational outcomes. *British Journal of Educational Psychology* 74:141–153.

128. Bronfenbrenner, U. 1979. *The ecology of human development: Experiments by nature and design.* Cambridge: Harvard University Press.

129. National Association for the Education of Young Children. 2005. *NAEYC early childhood program standards and accreditation criteria,* 11. Washington, D.C.: NAEYC.

130. Bredekamp, S., and C. Copple, eds. 1997. *Developmentally appropriate practice in early childhood programs,* rev. ed. Washington, D.C.: NAEYC.

131. Ghazvini, A. S., and C. A. Readdick. 1994. Parent–caregiver communication and quality of care in diverse child care settings. *Early Childhood Research Quarterly* 9:207–222.

132. Roach, M. A., Y. Kim, D. B. Adams, D. A. Riley, and D. Edie. 2006. How can we strengthen families through early care and education? *Wisconsin Child Care Research Partnership, Issue Brief #17.* Madison: University of Wisconsin–Extension.

133. McCartney, K., E. Dearing, and B. A. Taylor. 2003. Is high-quality child care an intervention for children from low-income families? Paper presented at the Biennial Meeting of the Society for Research in Child Development. Tampa, Fl.

134. Riley, D., and B. Schmidt. 1993. *Evaluation of Satellite Family Child Care.* Madison: University of Wisconsin-Extension.

135. Powers, J. 2005. *Parent-friendly early learning: Tips and strategies for working well with parents,* 2–4. St. Paul: Redleaf Press.

136. Keyser, J. 2006. *From parents to partners: Building a family-centered early childhood program,* 12. St. Paul: Redleaf Press.

137. Cochran, M., and S. Niego. 2004. Parenting and social networks. In *Handbook of parenting,* edited by M. Bornstein. Mahwah, N.J.: Lawrence Erlbaum Associates.

138. Crockenberg, S. 1981. Infant irritability, mother responsiveness, and social support influences on the security of infant–mother attachment. *Child Development* 52:857–865.

139. Green, S. 2003. Reaching out to fathers: An examination of staff efforts that lead to greater father involvement in early childhood programs. *Early Childhood Research & Practice* 5 (2):1–17.

140. Salzinger, S., S. Kaplan, and C. Artemyeff. 1983. Mothers' personal social networks and child maltreatment. *Journal of Abnormal Psychology* 92:68–76.

141. Cochran, M., and S. Niego. 2004. Parenting and social networks. In *Handbook of parenting*, ed. M. Bornstein. Mahwah, N.J.: Lawrence Erlbaum.

142. Hamilton, M. E., M. A. Roach, and D. A. Riley. 2003. Moving toward family-centered early care and education: The past, the present, and a glimpse of the future. *Early Childhood Education Journal* 30 (4):225–232.

143. Holloway, S. D., and B. Fuller. 1999. Families and child care: Divergent viewpoints. *Annals of the American Academy of Political and Social Science* 563:98–115.

144. Bennett, T. 2006. Future teachers forge family connections. *Young Children* 61:22–27.

145. Kontos, S., H. Raikes, and A. Woods. 1983. Early childhood staff attitudes toward their parent clientele. *Child Care Quarterly* 12:45–58.

146. Lopez, M. E., and S. Dorros. 1999. *Family-centered child care.* ERIC Document no. ED434745. Cambridge, Mass.: Harvard Family Research Project.

147. Kontos, S., and L. Dunn. 1989. Attitudes of caregivers, maternal experiences with day care, and children's development. *Journal of Applied Developmental Psychology* 10:37–51.

148. Powell, D. R. 2003. Relations between families and early childhood programs. In *Connecting with parents in the early years*, edited by J. Mendoza, L. J. Katz, A. S. Robertson, and D. Rosenberg, 146. Champaign: University of Illinois at Urbana-Champaign.

149. Hamilton, M. E., M. A. Roach, and D. A. Riley. 2003. Moving toward family-centered early care and education: The past, the present, and a glimpse of the future. *Early Childhood Education Journal* 30:227.

150. Young, K. T., K. Davis, C. Schoen, and S. Parker. 1998. Listening to parents: A national survey of parents with young children. *Archives of Pediatrics & Adolescent Medicine* 152:255–262.

151. Hoover-Dempsey, K. V., and H. M. Sandler. 1997. Why do parents become involved in their children's education? *Review of Educational Research* 67:3–42.

152. Powell, D. R. 1998. Reweaving parents into the fabric of early childhood programs. *Young Children* 53:60–67.

153. Hamilton, M. E., M. A. Roach, and D. A. Riley. 2003. Families as partners in centers for excellence. *Child Care Information Exchange* 150:14–16, 18.

154. Hamilton, M. E., M. A. Roach, and D. A. Riley. 2003. Families as partners in centers for excellence. *Child Care Information Exchange* 150:14.

155. Roach, M. A., Y. Kim, D. B. Adams, D. A. Riley, and D. Edie. 2006. How can we strengthen families through early care and education? *Wisconsin Child Care Research Partnership, Issue Brief #17.* Madison: University of Wisconsin–Extension.

156. Endsley, R. C., and P. A. Minish. 1991. Parent–staff communication in day care centers during morning and afternoon transitions. *Early Childhood Research Quarterly* 6:119–135.

157. Ghazvini, A. S., and C. A. Readdick. 1994. Parent–caregiver communication and quality of care in diverse child care settings. *Early Childhood Research Quarterly* 9:207–222.

158. Gonzalez-Mena, J., and D. Widmeyer Eyer. 2004. *Infants, toddlers, and caregivers: A curriculum of respectful, responsive care and education,* 6th ed. New York: McGraw-Hill.

159. Hamilton, M. E., M. A. Roach, and D. A. Riley. 2003. Moving toward family-centered early care and education: The past, the present, and a glimpse of the future. *Early Childhood Education Journal* 30:231–232.

160. Epstein, J. L., M. G. Sanders, B. S. Simon, K. Clark Salinas, N. R. Jansorn, and F. L. Van Voorhis. 2002. *School, family, and community partnerships: Your handbook for action,* 2nd ed. Thousand Oaks, Calif.: Corwin; Epstein, J. L. 2006. Families, schools, and community partnerships. *Young Children* 61:40.

Index

About the authors

Dave Riley, PhD, began working as a Head Start assistant teacher in East Los Angeles in 1972 and has several years of experience as a Head Start educational consultant. He has taught at the community college and university levels, including the last two decades at the University of Wisconsin-Madison, where he is the Rothermel-Bascom Professor of Human Development and the Associate Dean for Outreach of the School of Human Ecology. His published research focuses on early care and education, parent–child relations, and parenting education. He was the codirector of the Wisconsin Early Childhood Excellence Initiative and the Wisconsin Child Care Research Partnership.

Robert R. San Juan, PhD, has three years of experience as an early childhood educator. In his research he investigates young children's peer relationships, particularly the friendships of preschool-aged children. He has taught child development and parent–child relationship courses at the university level, and he currently works as a researcher at Purdue University on projects implementing interventions targeted at improving school readiness, particularly early literacy skills, in Head Start children.

Joan Klinkner has twenty years of experience working directly with young children, primarily in a teacher-training lab preschool at a community college. For the past twenty years she has taught college courses in early childhood education and is currently an instructor at Northeast Wisconsin Technical College in Green Bay, Wisconsin. She is the author of numerous articles on child care issues, specializing in infant-toddler development and early childhood mentoring. Joan has a master's degree in early childhood education from Concordia University in St. Paul, Minnesota. She was the recipient of the 2005 outstanding service award for the Wisconsin Division for Early Childhood and Wisconsin Early Childhood Associations.

Ann Ramminger worked for nine years as a Head Start teacher, director, and administrator. She has experienced the accreditation system of the National Association for the Education of Young Children (NAEYC) as both a director of an accredited program and as a validator. Ann has worked with many communities in Wisconsin around early childhood collaboration issues, such as four-year-old kindergarten and using the Wisconsin Model Early Learning Standards as common language to improve services for children. She has a BS in early childhood education with graduate work in early childhood mentoring, reflective practice, and the family service credential.

Mary Carns has worked as an early childhood teacher, movement teacher for preschoolers, and observational data collector for child care research. Most recently she has been employed as a research specialist at the Center for Genetic Medicine at Northwestern University. She has an MS in human development and family studies from the University of Wisconsin-Madison.

Kathleen Burns has six years of experience as an early childhood lead teacher. She also works as a teacher trainer and parent educator, and has been a CDA adviser since 2001. She has served as a member of the Child Care Advisory Council for Wisconsin state government and is a board member for the Kenosha Association for the Education of Young Children. Kathy is also a "child care partner" on Kenosha County's Special Quest team, which supports the inclusion of young children with special needs in early education settings by offering training and technical support. Kathy has a bachelor of science degree.

Mary Roach, PhD, is a child development specialist with the University of Wisconsin-Extension and was the codirector of the Wisconsin Early Childhood Excellence Initiative and the Wisconsin Child Care Research Partnership. She began her career as a preschool teacher but has worked as a researcher for the past two decades, studying the quality of caregiver–child interaction as it relates to outcomes for children (particularly children at risk for developmental delay), the role of families in supporting children's development, and early care and education policies.

Cindy Clark-Ericksen has nine years of experience as an early childhood education teacher, including a year as Head Teacher of the High/Scope Demonstration Preschool in Ypsilanti, Michigan. She has also worked as the staff development coordinator and director of an early care and education program, as a community liaison for a four-year-old kindergarten program, and as a college instructor for courses in early childhood education. For eight years she was the family living educator for the Cooperative Extension Service in her rural county. She has an MA degree in human development from Pacific Oaks College, and an MS in marital and family therapy from the University of Wisconsin-Stout. She currently works as a family therapist.